MURDER IN KENT

Born in Hampstead in 1949, Philip MacDougall graduated from Lancaster University and moved to Kent in the early seventies, where he took up a teaching post in the Medway towns. Eight books about Kent's history have already appeared under his name, and he contributes regularly to a number of magazines. He is additionally an historical advisor to the Chatham Historic Dockyard Trust and runs his own historical research agency. Fascinated by the mysterious and unusual in his adopted county, he lives in Rochester with his wife and son.

By the same author

The Hoo Peninsula Story
The Chatham Dockyard Story
Chatham Built Warships
Royal Dockyards
A First Picture Book of Old Chatham
Mysteries on the High Seas
A Second Picture Book of Old Chatham
A Third Picture Book of Old Chatham
The Book of Medway

MURDER IN KENT

PHILIP MACDOUGALL

ROBERT HALE · LONDON

First published in Great Britain 1989

Robert Hale Limited
Clerkenwell House
Clerkenwell Green
London EC1R 0HT

British Library Cataloguing in Publication Data

MacDougall, Philip
Murder in Kent : a new look at notorious cases.
1. Kent. Murder. History
I. Title
364.1′523′094223

ISBN 0–7090–3827–5

Photoset in Palatino by
Derek Doyle & Associates, Mold, Clwyd.
Printed in Great Britain by
St Edmundsbury Press Ltd, Bury St Edmunds, Suffolk.
Bound by WBC Bookbinders Limited.

Contents

Acknowledgements

The writing of this book would not have been possible without the help of a great number of people. In particular I would like to thank Detective Superintendent Roger Hext and WPC Ann Palfreman of Police Headquarters at Maidstone, together with members of the county's Fingerprint Bureau. All were kind enough to provide help with certain technical details. In addition, I would like to thank Harold Gough (of Herne Bay), Fred Brisley (whose police duties once included motor patrol) and the staff of various Kent libraries, but especially those of Ashford, Chatham, Gillingham, Gravesend and Herne Bay. Finally, I must reserve special thanks to my wife, who carefully read and commented upon the book as it went through each of the stages leading towards final publication.

MURDER IN KENT

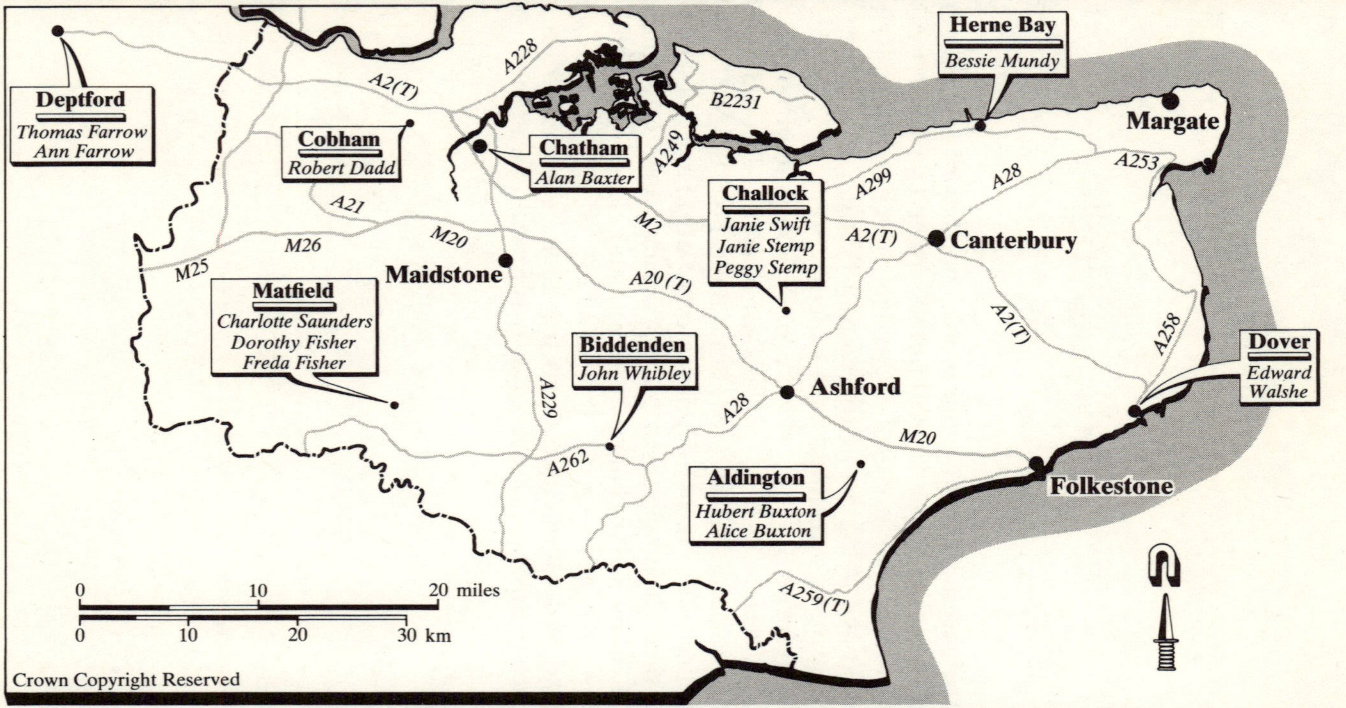

THE NAMES OF THE VICTIMS ARE SHOWN IN ITALIC BELOW THE PLACE NAMES

Introduction

Murder, although a hideous and terrible act, never ceases to fascinate. Thankfully, for most of us, the motives which drive a person to such an act are impossible to understand. Maybe this is the real reason it retains such interest. As with science fiction, it is a journey into the unknown.

In Kent, a county which is normally seen as being rather peaceful and possessing a relatively law-abiding population, murder has been committed on literally hundreds of occasions. Greed, love, envy, hatred and a dozen other emotions have all been used to explain the inexplicable. For this book I have carefully selected a range of murders that have taken place within the county, leaning heavily upon those which are, in some way, different. Whilst a few are reasonably well known, others are rarely mentioned. All, however, are thoroughly researched, with new information added and a number of previous factual errors corrected. With regard to the several sampled conversations included within the pages of this book, most are drawn from contemporary newspaper accounts. In one or two cases I have found it necessary to add an interrogative or linking phrase which seems to have been omitted from that original account. All else is historically accurate.

Although the book is entitled *Murder in Kent,* some readers may be surprised to see the inclusion of Deptford in one of the chapters. This is no mistake. Although Deptford has now been incorporated into London, historically it is part of Kent. In defining the boundaries for this book, I deliberately included traditional Kent rather than present-day county boundaries.

– 1 –
Artistic Licence,
Cobham,
1843

Shortly before seven o'clock on the morning of Tuesday 29 August 1843, Charles Lester and his uncle Abraham Lester were passing through Cobham Woods. The purpose of their journey was strictly business. Both of them were Rochester butchers and intended spending the day at Wrotham market, where they hoped to pick up livestock at bargain prices.

So far they had been travelling for about an hour. Having left the city of Rochester via its medieval bridge, they had then entered the village of Strood. From here, they had joined the ancient trackway of Watling Street, following its course as it ascends a shallow hill that levels out somewhere close to Shorne. Continuing in a London-bound direction, it had not taken them long to reach the narrow, leafy gladed trackway of Halfpence Lane. In summer, when the roads were dry, this served as a useful short cut to that more distant village of Wrotham. In all, the entire journey would take about two hours.

Since leaving Watling Street, they had seen few other travellers. In fact, Halfpence Lane appeared totally devoid of life, something that was in direct contrast to scenes already witnessed in Rochester and Strood. Both communities, despite the earliness of the hour, seemed fully engaged in preparing for the coming day, for two important events clashed during that final week in August.

Strood, which had then a population to be counted in hundreds rather than thousands, was holding its annual fair, sited on land close to the High Street. The previous evening had witnessed a variety of traders, tricksters and entertainers desperate in their desire to please an ever-sceptical public. As always, it was the drinking-booths that had proved the most successful in fleecing the unwary of their hard-earned cash. Many an inebriated soul was spending part of the night huddled in some dark corner sleeping off a final half-dozen or so pints. It was this latter group, together with those who had lost heavily in the gambling-booths, who were now beginning to stir. Although tired and awkward, they did create a feeling of momentum in that early morning hour.

Whilst Strood had already embarked upon a short season of merriment, Rochester was about to witness something much more lavish. On the nearby Chatham Lines, a huge military display was planned for the afternoon. Thousands had already descended upon the cathedral city, aware that its open streets would provide them with a bed for the night. As with the inebriates and gamblers of Strood, the bright morning sun had also encouraged them to make an early start to the day.

From the excitement and bustle of Rochester and Strood, the peacefulness of Halfpence Lane must have been a welcome relief to the Lesters, but as their horse-drawn cart approached the final bend that would take them into the village of Cobham, they noticed a sight that was reminiscent of daybreak in Strood. Just thirty yards from the road, the still body of a man could be seen lying face down in a small hollow.

The thirty-six-year-old Charles assumed, quite naturally, that the body was that of another victim of Strood fair and its drinking-booths. To his uncle he offered two possibilities: 'He's either dead or asleep.' But if he was a victim of the fair, he had certainly managed to walk some distance – a total of five miles. Puzzled by this curious incident, Charles decided to stop and have a closer look. After all, he might be in need of assistance.

As Charles stepped down from the road, passing through a gap in the trees, he could see that the man, who was wearing a carefully tailored black suit and green plaid waistcoat, was certainly very still. Upon trying to rouse him there was absolutely no response. At that point the truth finally dawned upon him.

'It seems he is dead!' he called back to his uncle.

'Come back!' was the anxious reply.

'Wait, I'll just have a closer look.'

It was just as he was about to pull the body over that Charles noticed another man, who was within hailing distance. This was George Briggs, a thirty-two-year-old shepherd who lived in Elsom Bottom.

'Do you know there's a dead man here?' Charles called out.

'No,' replied Briggs, who was slowly approaching the scene. 'I've been looking after sheep.'

Between them they turned the body over. The cause of death was immediately apparent. The fallen man had been knifed in several places. His coat was torn and a great quantity of blood was to be seen on both his face and hands. Between them Briggs and Lester agreed that the best course of action was to inform the village constable.

At this point the twentieth-century reader, nurtured on a diet of fast-action detective fiction, will probably expect the mounting of a massive police investigation that would encompass a widespread search of the area, house-to-house calls and the detaining of numerous suspects. In the event, nothing could be further from the truth. Policing methods in early nineteenth-century Kent were simply not designed for combating serious crime. In most villages the constable was little more than an amateur, having been appointed at the annual parish meeting from amongst those eligible to pay rates. In theory, each male villager was to take his turn in serving as constable, but the more affluent usually chose to pay someone else to serve in their place.

Because of a simple lack of training, combined with an inability to call upon anyone else with greater experience, William Dawes, full-time tailor and part-time constable, was soon out of his depth. Upon Charles Lester's calling at his house and reporting that he had found a body, Dawes made the first of several mistakes. He simply allowed the Rochester butcher to continue his journey, failing to take even a simple statement. If nothing else, he should have asked the Lesters if they had seen anyone acting in a suspicious manner or if they had touched anything in the immediate vicinity of the body.

Upon Constable Dawes' arrival at the scene of the crime, he immediately blundered around in a haphazard and disorganized manner. Nevertheless, he did manage to uncover a few items connected with the murder. First and foremost was the discovery of a clasp-knife lying close to the body and showing every sign of having been used in the attack. The constable then went on to examine the body, noting that the throat of the deceased had been cut, whilst there were stab wounds to the chest.

In an effort to identify the victim, Dawes also searched the body, discovering a pair of spectacles, a comb, a gold watch and a small sum of money. Clearly, so it would appear, the motive had not been that of robbery, although it was possible that the murderer had been disturbed during the attack and had then chosen to flee the area. Neither possibility seems to have occurred to Dawes.

However, the real failure of Constable Dawes was in not properly organizing several villagers who had come to gawp at this tragedy in their midst. Wandering around the murder site and nearby road, they were probably responsible for trampling over several clues that might have included footprints and splashes of blood. It also seems likely that it was one of these inquisitive villagers who discovered a bloodstained razor blade. For his part, Dawes later admitted that he had no idea who had found it, nor even its precise location.

The discovery of blood on a nearby stile provided further evidence of Dawes' inability to carry out the task he had been set. With the marks shaped like a hand and clearly made by someone climbing over the stile, Dawes made the incredible assumption that they had been left there by Charles Lester immediately after he had found the body. It was a mistake that could so easily have been avoided. If Dawes had taken a simple statement from Lester, he would have discovered that the man from Rochester had left no such mark. This same statement would also have told the constable that all the blood on the victim had been dry even when first discovered, so telling him that the murder had taken place several hours earlier.

In fact, proper use of this particular discovery would have been extremely useful in tracking down the culprit. As the stile was on a pathway leading away from the village, it was clear that the murderer was heading towards Watling Street. Secondly, of course, if the murderer had such excessive amounts of blood on one hand, it also seems likely that it had spread to the clothes he or she was wearing. Again, this would have been useful in composing a description of the murderer that would help in an early arrest. Constable Dawes, in failing to take a statement from Charles Lester, was not in a position to use either clue.

Amongst the villagers who had joined Dawes at the scene of the murder was John Adams, a waiter at the Ship

Inn. Somewhat more astute than Dawes, he realized by the coldness of the body that the murder must have happened some hours earlier. Even more important, Adams recognized the victim, naming him as Robert Dadd. The previous evening, at about six o'clock, the man had called at the Ship, requesting a bed for the night. Although no rooms were available, the Ship being too small to offer such a service, Adams did arrange for accommodation in a nearby cottage.

Adams already knew Robert Dadd prior to his turning up at the Ship. Choosing to give Dawes some background information, Adams indicated that the Dadds had once been an established Chatham family, with Robert a retired chemist who had owned a shop in the town's High Street. He went on to point out that Robert Dadd had played an important part in Chatham's social life. A founder member of the Chatham and Rochester Literary and Philosophical Institute, he had also been politically active. During the years which led up to the passing of the Great Reform Bill of 1832, he had proved himself an enthusiastic campaigner for the extension of political rights to the middle classes. However, in concluding this potted biography, Adams mentioned that he had not seen Robert Dadd for about ten years. Apparently he had taken his family to London in 1834.

Although these details of Robert Dadd's background were of interest, none of it compared with one other item of information that was now produced. Arriving at Cobham, Robert Dadd had not been alone: he had been accompanied by his twenty-six-year-old son, Richard. Following their arrival at the Ship, both men had taken refreshments before going out for a late-evening walk. According to Adams, they had left the inn at about nine o'clock. He was not sure which direction they had taken, but assumed they had gone to the park. This, an area of open ground that surrounds Cobham Hall, the palatial residence of Lord Darnley, was a popular recreational area often frequented by those who knew Cobham.

In his assumption as to where the two had gone, Adams was absolutely correct. From later evidence we now know that they had carefully skirted the perimeter of the park, passing behind Cobham Hall before heading back to the village via Halfpence Lane. As they approached a hollow that stood adjacent to the lane, Robert decided that he needed to relieve himself. Facing away from his son, he started to undo his front trouser buttons.

It was now that tragedy struck. In a moment of uncontrolled frenzy, Richard attacked his father. Removing a specially purchased rigging- (or clasp-) knife from his pocket, he came at his father from behind. Throwing his left arm across the older man's chest, he not only held him still but successfully pinioned both his arms. Using his other hand, Richard pulled the knife across the left side of his father's neck. Although it resulted in a great deal of blood, this first wound was to prove only superficial.

Robert, although taken off guard, responded immediately. Freeing one of his hands, he made a grab for the knife, and the two of them fell to the ground. During the next few seconds, Richard used his left hand to throw a few vicious punches, each of them catching his father in the face. Eventually, weakened by the loss of blood, Robert Dadd fell back, allowing his son to regain the initiative. Rolling on top of his father, he drove the knife deep into his shoulder. Again, the wound was not fatal, but Robert, now in considerable pain, was beginning to lose the will to fight. The result was two further stabs, each to the chest. The second of these, missing the heart by inches, entered into the lung and pierced it in two places. Within seconds Robert Dadd had ceased to exist. He had been murdered by his own son.

Having carried out this act of treachery, Richard Dadd

made his escape over that nearby stile, his bloody handprint serving as clear evidence of the direction of his escape. Entering Halfpence Lane, it seems likely that he ran on to Watling Street, where he must have been given a lift by a passing traveller. Leastways, it was later reported that Richard had entered the City of Rochester by about 10p.m.

To William Dawes, now masterminding the investigations into Kent's most serious crime for at least a decade, few of these facts were known. Of only one thing could the village constable be certain: this was the clear fact of Richard's presence in the locality of the murder. There was also the near-certainty that he would be able to throw some light on the events that had occurred. The only problem, from Dawes' point of view, was that the man appeared to be missing. In view of the limited information available, it was perfectly reasonable to assume that Richard Dadd might also have been murdered.

With this thought in his mind, Dawes now took a positive decision. A general search of the park and nearby road must be undertaken. Volunteers were sought from amongst those who lived in the area, everyone detailed to look out for a second body.

Whilst one may accept that Dawes had taken a correct decision, this should not have precluded his taking at least one other course of action. He should, as a matter of urgency, have sent a message to some of the local magistrates. They, after all, were the next line of authority and had the right to order a 'hue and cry' by which means the entire county would have been alerted to the existence of an escaping felon. It was this further error on the part of Dawes that allowed Richard Dadd to reach Dover, where he subsequently hired an open boat that conveyed him to Calais.

Temporarily leaving this fruitless and inevitably time-consuming search, it is worth having a more detailed look at Richard Dadd. Born in August 1817, he was the fourth child of Robert's first marriage. Educated in the Medway towns, he proved to be an exceptionally talented artist. In fact, it was his outstanding skills that encouraged Robert to make that move to London in 1834. After all, however capable his son might be, no one was really going to notice him in Chatham.

The move to London paid off. In 1837 the talented youngster was admitted to the Royal Academy Schools, where he was to gain a reputation as a potentially brilliant artist. A great many of those who worked with him were highly impressed, seeing Dadd as one who would soon gain national fame. The great Victorian artist Frith, who was a contemporary of Dadd at the Royal Academy, was one who freely praised this artist in the making. In his biography, Frith was to write: 'Dadd was my superior in all respects; he drew infinitely better than I did.'

Going on to gain for himself an outstanding reputation amongst the *cognoscenti*, Richard was given an important commission in 1842. He was asked by Sir Thomas Phillips, a South Wales solicitor, to accompany him on a forthcoming 'Grand Tour' of Europe and North Africa. In an age before the invention of the portable camera, it was quite normal for the affluent to patronize artists in this way, ensuring that they would have their memories placed on canvas. For Richard Dadd, it was a unique opportunity to further his career.

Leaving Britain in July of that year, they travelled across Belgium, Germany, Switzerland and Italy, stopping only to take in art galleries, archaeological remains and breathtaking scenery. Within a month they had reached the Italian coastal port of Ancona, the tour having proceeded at such a pace that it would have defeated all but the most dedicated. So rapid was their progress that Richard was given few opportunities to make sketches, casting most of these early experiences to memory. In later years he was frequently to introduce Alpine mountain scenes, turreted castles and Italian sea ports in the most imaginative of his works.

From Ancona they crossed the Mediterranean, heading for the Greek peninsula and the opportunity of absorbing this early cultural civilization at its very roots. Again, the adopted pace was essentially rapid, and the following month saw them visiting Corfu, Patras, Delphi and then Athens. It was only with their arrival at this bastion of European civilization that things began to slow down, Phillips setting aside a week for the Parthenon and other Athenian antiquities.

Yet, despite this obsession with visiting such an array of wonders in so short a period of time, Richard Dadd's enthusiasm was far from diminished. From Corfu he wrote of his 'eyes and mouth wide open, swallowing with insatiable appetite the everlasting succession of picturesque characters'. Considering all that he saw as ideal for the artist, he described the general population as including '… a large assortment of pompous ruffians, splendid savages … I never saw such an assemblage of deliciously villainous faces: they grinned, glowered and exhibited every variety of curiosity. Oh such expressions! Oh such heads! Enough to turn the brain of an artist.'

Travelling by boat, horse, mule, foot and camel, the pace again quickened upon leaving Greece, with the two of them taking in Smyrna and Istanbul before directing themselves to the Holy Land. But it was not long before Richard was showing early signs of impending madness – a madness that climaxed with that frenzied attack upon his father. In a letter to Frith, written whilst journeying between Jaffa and Alexandria, Richard included these lines that were to prove prophetic: 'At times the excitement of these scenes has been enough to turn the brain of an ordinary weak-minded person like myself, and often I have lain down at night with my imagination so full of wild vagaries that I have really and truly doubted of my own sanity. The heat of the day, perhaps, contributed somewhat to this, or the motion of riding is also another reason for this unusual activity of the fancy.'

Christmas saw them in Cairo. It was here that Richard entered into a more severe spate of madness. Believing himself taken over by Osiris, an ancient god of that city, he declared it to be his intention to rid the world of all its evil. Viewing this as a temporary aberration that lasted no more than a few days, his companion put it down to sunstroke and credited the affair as having no real importance. But Richard was certainly aware that his inner being was under attack and desperately tried to fight this nightmare journey into madness. Upon starting the return journey to Britain, he wrote of the sea passage to Malta: 'I never passed six more miserable days. I scarcely know – perhaps I should say that I am perfectly ignorant of – the cause of the nervous depression that I experienced.'

In Rome he was overtaken by the first of several uncontrollable impulses. Seeing the Pope as the epitome of the world's evil, he determined upon the destruction of the august personage. That he failed in this objective was merely the result of the high level of security that existed in the Vatican City.

One man who was in constant danger at this time was Sir Thomas Phillips. Those final weeks of the tour were characterized by Richard's increasing hostility towards his patron, the two of them frequently arguing. Not that all this should be blamed on Richard Dadd. Phillips was an egotistical character who wanted everything his way. Having demanded that the tour should proceed with such rapidity, he now blamed Richard for undertaking such a small number of sketches. When they eventually came to blows, in Paris, Phillips was lucky to escape with his life.

Upon Richard Dadd's returning to Britain, his various friends and relatives were quick to notice a severe change in his personality. Whereas William Frith had once found him 'charming in companionship' and having 'amiable qualities', Richard was now hateful, argumentative and suspicious of all those around him. Frequently he would lock himself away, choosing to have little to do with his former friends.

Samuel Carter Hall, editor of the *Art Journal,* made a number of visits to Richard's London flat during the weeks immediately following his return from the 'Grand Tour'. In his later autobiography he was to comment: 'I could never tell why, but, although I liked him much, I had always in his presence a sense of apprehension. One evening, at my house, he was more than usually gloomy, spoke little, but his eyes seemed to roll about the assembled group. It was whispered by more than one, "What is the matter with Dadd?" After his arrest a paper was found containing outline portraits of all the artists then present, with a dash of red paint across the throat of each.'

Whilst Hall may have had 'a sense of apprehension' when in Richard's company, others were totally unnerved by him. His landlady, in particular, would often hear him ranting and raging in his room and on occasions she would glimpse a knife waved under the door. She would, of course, have been even more unnerved if she had entered the room, for she would probably have come across him working on that outline picture of his artist friends, each with the dash of red that represented their throats having been cut.

For sustenance, Richard seems to have survived on a diet consisting entirely of eggs washed down with beer. Leastways, when his room was later searched, it was found to contain over 300 eggs, his furniture and carpeting entirely covered in shells.

At first, Robert Dadd refused to believe that there was anything wrong with his son, considering his behaviour to be a result of severe sunstroke. Eventually he agreed to consult Dr Sutherland of St Luke's Asylum. Given a description of Richard's symptoms, it soon became apparent to Sutherland, a specialist in treating madness, that potentially he was an extremely dangerous person. Although he did not put a name to the illness, which is now referred to as paranoid schizophrenia, he did urge that Richard be committed to an asylum.

For such a caring father, this was a quite unacceptable solution. Instead, he determined to bring Richard back into his own home, possibly giving thought to the employment of a nurse. But these plans were little advanced when Richard called on his father, suggesting a visit to Cobham Park. This was an area known to both of them, the family having frequently visited the park when they lived at Chatham. Because of its association with an earlier period of happiness, Robert agreed to the suggestion, believing that his son would readily unburden his mind in such an environment.

It was clear that Robert was completely unaware of the danger that now confronted him. Others, however, were less certain about how safe he would be. In particular his eldest daughter, Mary-Ann, made considerable efforts to persuade him not to accompany Richard, fearing that something awful might happen. Failing in these endeavours, she hastily scribbled a note to her brother Stephen, asking him to look after their father. At the time, Stephen was already in the Medway area, having taken accommodation at Strood, to watch the forthcoming military manœuvres at Chatham. Unfortunately, by the time the letter arrived, Robert Dadd had already been murdered by his crazed son.

The eventual realization that the murder had almost certainly been committed by Richard did not reach the ears of Cobham's village constable until later in the week. By that time an exhaustive search of the park had been completed, whilst a long-delayed message had also been dispatched to several of the local magistrates. At this point, a county-wide search should certainly have been initiated, but the magistracy seemed to take a lackadaisical approach similar to that previously adopted by William Dawes. Instead of extending the search as widely as possible, they chose to limit the 'hue and cry' to the two North Kent towns of Gravesend and Rochester.

Not surprisingly, the inability of the forces of law and order to come to grips with the situation resulted in considerable criticism being levelled at the whole system. In the words of one local newspaper, the *Kentish Independent*: 'Crime might have been added to crime; and sorrow heaped upon sorrow; when a slight exertion of active ability would have been sufficient to ensure the safety of the community from all the dread, as far as the unhappy maniac in question is concerned. As it is, the next hour may bring intelligence of new scenes of blood and horror.'

In fact, the most positive move in the search to apprehend Richard was taken not by the forces of law and order but by the unhappy family of which Robert had once been the head. Within hours of hearing of that dreadful event at Cobham, they had ordered the printing of a number of handbills that offered a £10 reward for anyone 'finding or securing' Richard Dadd.

Of course, by the time anyone read these handbills, Richard was safely ensconced in France. Here he might well have remained had it not been for his own crazed imaginings. Whilst travelling on a coach through Valence, he started to hear voices which ordered him to kill his fellow passenger. At first he resisted these instructions, but he finally decided that it must be the will of Osiris. Producing a razor, he lunged at the man's throat, inflicting four painful cuts. As with the initial attack on his father, they did not prove fatal, the victim on this occasion managing to overpower Richard.

Upon the arrival of the coach at the next town, the local *gendarmerie* were informed of the attack, and Richard was instantly arrested. Surprisingly, he made no attempt to conceal his identity, freely admitting to the earlier attack upon his father. The immediate outcome was that the French authorities certified him insane and committed him to an asylum where he was to remain until the following summer.

The British Home Secretary was determined upon Richard's extradition, considering it essential that he be brought to trial. In order to ensure his safe return, two officers from London's newly established Metropolitan Police were ordered to France in July 1844. Prior to their departure they had first to visit Rochester, where, on 26 June, they collected warrants for Richard's arrest.

Although potentially a complex procedure, Richard Dadd's extradition was performed with a degree of efficiency that had previously eluded this entire affair. Delayed for only a couple of days in Paris, the two officers, aided by a *gendarme,* collected Richard from the Claremont Asylum on the evening of 26 July, returning to Britain on a steamer from Boulogne.

In the meantime, the Rochester magistrates had been apprised of Richard's likely arrival in the city sometime on the afternoon of 29 July. For this reason they were already in session, with a sizeable crowd packed into the public gallery. Hoping to be entertained, the worthy citizenry of Rochester were not disappointed. Shortly after the appointed time, a truly frightening figure strode through the door. Tall, muscular and with long bushy hair, Richard appeared to these spectators as a representative of that same evil force which it had been his intention to destroy.

Carefully studying all those present, his dark, staring eyes eventually fixed themselves on one particular member of the public.

'He's the murderer,' Richard declared in a deep

booming voice. 'He's the murderer. He said, "You bloody old villain"!'

The purpose of this first court appearance was simply to remand him until the following Monday, by which time the various witnesses could be assembled. On being asked whether he had any objections, Richard restrained himself from making a further outburst, calmly replying 'No' to the question.

However, one final demonstration of the prisoner's insanity occurred just as the magistrates were about to retire. Marching to the head of the courtroom, he fixedly stared at each magistrate in turn.

'He said he should do that,' he declared without further explanation.

Richard's appearance before this same court just seven days later was to prove even more entertaining for those who managed to obtain admission. Certainly a great many used personal influence to gain a reserved seat, for the list of those present reads like a Medway *Who's Who*. Included in their number were the Mayor of Rochester, several Church dignitaries and a sprinkling of Army officers. One local newspaper, the *Rochester Gazette*, in reporting the trial, duly listed the names of many of these 'spectators' as if it were the first night of a new play at the local Theatre Royal on Star Hill.

Amongst the first group of witnesses to be called was William Dawes. After taking the oath he proceeded to outline events that had occurred in Cobham almost twelve months earlier.

'On the morning of 29 August, in consequence of information received from Mr C. Lester', the constable formally related, 'I went to Cobham Park and found a body of a man on the grass.'

The courtroom had fallen into hushed silence. No one wanted to miss a single word. Then, as the constable described the state of the body, Richard suddenly called out:

'I did not!'

'There were holes cut in the shirt and waistcoat,' Dawes continued.

'No, no,' the prisoner interrupted once again.

'I have the clothes,' was the slightly unnerved reply from Dawes.

'No, oh no,' from the prisoner.

'I have also the knife and razor.'

'I tell you, I never did it.'

Such interruptions were to continue for most of the hearing. Sometimes Richard would attempt to state his innocence and at other times he would contradict those earlier declarations. This sad and pathetic spectacle continued, to the obvious delight of the assembled 'audience'.

Following Dawes onto the witness stand was William Saunders, a Gravesend surgeon who had carried out a post mortem on the body of Robert Dadd. Giving an account of what he had discovered, he mentioned that there had been a great deal of blood on the face and hands.

'I used no more violence than was necessary,' claimed the man who had only a few moments earlier stated he had had nothing to do with the murder.

'I found the lips closed,' continued the surgeon.

'Oh what stories,' Richard responded.

'I found bruises on the wrist,' from Saunders.

'I didn't do it!'

'The inner garments were wet with blood and there were holes cut in the waistcoat.'

By now Richard appeared to be sweating profusely. One of the magistrates turned and asked if he wanted a drink of water.

'I never drink water,' Richard replied. 'I only stabbed him once.'

'The pleura, lining the interior of the ribs,' continued

Saunders, 'was punctured in two places ...'

'I tell you I never did it!' came yet one more interruption.

'... although there was only one external wound,' continued Saunders with a voice that was beginning to weaken under the strain of the moment.

'Could you speak louder?' asked the chairman of the bench.

'I can hear,' declared Richard, who was clearly under the impression that it was all for his benefit.

In a similar manner, this trial of summary jurisdiction continued. Another witness called was Eliza Coleman, a chambermaid at Rochester's Crown Inn. She recalled an incident that had occurred on the day of the murder.

'On Monday night, the last night of Strood fair, I remember a gentleman coming in to wash his hands. I showed him into a room upstairs.'

For a short period of time, Richard chose to let this witness continue giving her evidence. Amongst other things, she mentioned the state of the wash-hand basin once he had finished. However, she was not certain about the colour of the water.

'It was very dark,' she replied to a question from the bench. 'But I could not tell with blood or dirt.'

'I took one of your towels,' admitted the prisoner. 'I took it because it had blood on it.'

This outburst occurred shortly after Eliza had indicated that Richard had ordered a post-chaise to take him to Sittingbourne.

'I tell you I did not do it,' he insisted. 'I never did it!'

As the trial proceeded, Richard continued with these interruptions, most of them totally contradictory. At one point his solicitor, feeling that no progress was being made, put his hands to his head in a gesture of despair.

'Brown, put your hand down!' came a sharp rebuke from Richard. 'If you are not ashamed of yourself, I am not.'

Following evidence from Frederick Shaw, one of the two

Metropolitan police officers who had brought Richard back from France, the magistrates chose to retire in order to discuss their decision. During this short recess, Richard continued to call out in a less than coherent fashion. For the safety of those present it was decided that he should be temporarily removed from the courtroom. Upon the magistrates' returning, he was again brought in, being present to hear the chairman commit him to trial at the next assizes to be held in Maidstone.

'No, oh no!' responded the prisoner.

In the event, Richard Dadd was not required to make an appearance at the Maidstone Assizes. Instead, he was certified insane under the Criminal Lunatic Act and removed to Bethlem Hospital on 22 August 1844. Here he remained for the next twenty-two years of his life, before removal to the new and better-equipped establishment at Broadmoor. At both hospitals, he was able to continue his painting, being allowed free use of paints. As a result, he produced a number of outstanding paintings, some of them leaning heavily upon his early connections with Chatham and that ill-fated European tour.

At first he remained an unpredictable and violent patient, often jumping up and striking people for no apparent reason. In his later years he settled down, although upon admission to Broadmoor he was still described as 'dangerous to others'. In December 1877 the *World* carried an account of his life in the asylum:

> A recluse doing the honours of his modest unpretending abode; a pleasant visaged old man with a long and flowing snow white beard, with mild blue eyes that beam benignly through spectacles when in conversation ... At Christmastide a few hours suffice to produce a host of humorous cartoons, comical street figures, policeman, papas, merry children, clown and pantaloon; he will turn out as rapidly diagrams

> and illustrations for a lecture or entertainment. He has adorned and beautified the asylum walls; above all upon the asylum theatre he has lavished much decoration of a peculiarly florid kind, quaint arabesques, and lines painted in a medley of vivid colours …

At Broadmoor, Richard's life ended. Shortly before Christmas 1887 he contracted a serious disease of the lungs, and he died in Infirmary No. 4 on the eighth day of the new year. As was customary practice at Broadmoor, he was buried in the grounds of the hospital, the site marked by a numbered stone that has since been removed. From his sister Mary-Ann he received this epitaph: 'I am truly thankful to know him at rest, it is less grief to me, than it was to think of him in the changed condition in which he has lived for many years past, his life has been to me a living death.'

– 2 –
Death on a Railway Station,
Dover,
1868

The possibility that certain sections of the media may have some influence upon the levels of violent crime is frequently at the forefront of public attention. In recent years a great deal of concern has centred around the dangers of television, various critics suggesting that there is a link between the showing of violent programmes and a general increase of violence in society. Whilst available evidence is far from conclusive, most sociologists accept that children, in particular, behave differently after watching a programme that contains violence. Although this altered pattern of behaviour lasts for only a short time, it is not impossible that the viewing of a large number of excessively violent programmes might also have a long-term effect.

This general anxiety about the media is far from new. Over the years concerned individuals have put forward the view that juvenile delinquency is connected with US pulp magazines, music-hall melodramas and the ubiquitous 'penny dreadfuls' that were first published towards the end of the last century.

Perhaps the first expression of such fears came in the mid-nineteenth century, with the emergence of a type of newspaper known as a 'police sheet'. Produced on cheap-quality newsprint, it provided a constant stream of reports detailing various shocking crimes known to have occurred throughout the country. A typical issue would include a range of murders, a few mysterious deaths and a number of assaults. Most popular were stories that involved a woman as either victim or assailant. Often the articles seem to have been gleaned from various local papers, with the wording carefully altered to create a more sensational style. However, when compared with the twentieth-century 'gutter press', these newspapers seem remarkably constrained.

Apart from content, the most noticeable difference between a police sheet and an ordinary broadsheet newspaper was the use of front-page illustrations. Whereas *The Manchester Guardian*, *Times* and even *News of the World* had front pages reserved for adverts and occasional news stories, the police sheets used this part of the paper to ram home the nature of their content. Using highly evocative drawings they depicted, on a weekly basis, a range of human indignities that were designed to attract a mass readership from amongst an increasingly literate population.

One of the more avid readers of this species of newspaper was Thomas Wells. Eighteen years of age in 1868, he was employed by the London, Chatham & Dover Railway as a carriage-cleaner. Yearning for adventure and excitement, he spent most of his spare time engrossed in these papers, fascinated by the revealing illustrations and the detailed court reports that often went with them.

It is possible that he actually envied the temporary fame of the various criminals featured each week. Perhaps this is the real explanation for his act of murder, for, from the moment he fired the gun, Wells found himself elevated from anonymous reader to national infamy. Yet it was not so much the murder which caught public attention as the means by which Thomas Wells met his own demise. Although hanged, like thousands before him he was the first to be executed within the enclosed walls of a prison. All previous hangings had been carried out in public, with a crowd of blood-thirsty onlookers turning the whole affair into a gigantic party.

As for the events that brought Thomas Wells to the scaffold, these began at Dover during the early part of 1868. As a cleaner, most of his time was spent at the Priory station, where a number of sheds and sidings had been established for the company's teak-finished box-like carriages upon which he was normally employed. Throughout the summer months, both this and the Harbour station at Dover were amongst the busiest on the line. Several express trains ran direct from Victoria, bringing passengers for the Continental ferries or as holidaymakers to the town of Dover. Those who stayed for the summer season could enjoy the delights of a small promenade or take advantage of the bathing-machines lined up along the beach.

Despite the fact that Wells was employed upon one of the least rewarding tasks of railway work, it was not without prospects. The company frequently promoted those who showed signs of ambition, and Wells possibly thought of himself as future engine-driver or station master. This latter post was particularly sought-after, the company sometimes providing a small house close to its many stations.

Having been employed for about eighteen months at the Priory, Wells seems to have started out as a helpful and willing worker. But some noticed a distinct change in his character following an unfortunate accident that previous summer. As he passed between a carriage and an engine, one of them had begun to roll, trapping him between the buffers. Suffering both head and chest injuries, he had been taken home in a semi-conscious state. According to his parents, the accident had a lasting effect, Wells became aggressive and considerably less reliable.

The station master at the Priory was Edward Adolphus Walshe. To some he was a kindly man but to others a harsh disciplinarian. Wells, now seemingly reluctant to perform even the simplest tasks, was constantly in receipt of numerous threats and warnings. In April the young carriage-cleaner felt a special resentment at the latest set of instructions he had been given. Apart from normal routine work, he was also ordered to collect a cartful of manure and take it to the station master's garden. Almost certainly Walshe was exceeding his authority in this, but the more Wells complained, the more his superior refused to listen. Seeing the two alternatives as compliance or possible ejection from his job, Wells reluctantly collected the manure and placed it in the garden.

It was in that same week that Wells acquired a gun. It was an old-fashioned fowling-piece that required gun-powder and percussion caps.

At this stage, although he was furious at what he had been told to do, it is unlikely that Wells intended killing the station master. Maybe, when he received another set of disagreeable instructions, he would simply produce the gun and tell Walshe to think again.

On Thursday 29 April the aggrieved employee brought the gun to work. Finding a moment of spare time, he decided on some target practice. The bangs could be heard all over the station, with the superintendent furious at the incident. Having discovered who was responsible, he finally confronted Wells in the porters' room.

'I will have none of these tricks!' shouted Walshe as a final warning. Having spent some minutes in haranguing the youth, the station master stormed out, his face red with anger.

'I will let the old bugger have the contents of it!' Wells

threatened, knowing that he could be heard by others in the room.

'Don't be such a fool as that,' warned John Prescott, an engine-driver. 'If the old man was to hear, he would have you locked up for threatening.'

'I'll let the old bugger have it!' Wells continued. Clearly he was not going to be persuaded by the good sense of those around him.

Within a brief space of time Walshe re-entered the room. Having given thought to the incident, there was one matter that had yet to be cleared up.

'What did you do with the gun?'

'I flung it away!' Wells lied.

'I'm not done with you yet.' Then, going on to refer to the superintendent of the two Dover stations, Walshe continued, 'You will have to go down to see Mr Cox.'

This argument could have continued for much longer if it had not been interrupted by the timely arrival of the evening express from London. Due to stop for only a few minutes at the Priory station, it had yet to travel a further mile before terminating at the Harbour station. It was Wells' task to board the train each evening, remaining at the Harbour station to clean out the carriages prior to their use on the return train to Victoria.

'Come on, you must go,' Walshe was heard to say.

Both of them headed towards the train, with Wells slipping into the brake van. Walshe, a senior figure on the railway, opened the door of a conveniently empty first-class compartment. Instead of getting in, he seems to have had second thoughts, pushing the door shut and remaining on the platform.

Wells took this as his cue for another act of disobedience. As the train hissed and spluttered its way out of the station, he jumped free of the brake van, landing just short of the platform. Showing every sign of agitation, he now made his way towards the furious station master.

'Why?' came the the predictable interrogation. 'Why, didn't you stay on the train?'

'I'm not going down there to be made a bloody fool of!'

'I'll not accept this behaviour. It's gone too far. I'll telegraph to headquarters.'

At 6.30 the following morning Wells began his usual work in the carriage shed, the London express due to leave within two hours. It soon became clear that his dislike of Walshe had not changed in the slightest. He fell into conversation with a fellow employee, twelve-year-old Charles Sinclair of the 'loco' department, and their discussion came round to the station master and his clash with Wells.

'I thought you had to go down to the Harbour,' the youngster commented.

'I got into the brake, but the station master never got in, and when the train got as far as the tunnel, I got out.' A few moments later Wells added yet one more threat: 'If the old bugger says much more to me today, I'll shoot him!'

On two separate occasions, Wells had now threatened the station master. At the time, no one believed these to be anything more than bravado. Perhaps they might have thought otherwise if they had known that Wells had skipped off work during part of the morning to purchase 4 pence worth of gunpowder from an ironsmith's shop in Snargate Street.

It was not until late morning that Wells was finally called in to the station office, where he was confronted by Henry Cox. Also present for the interview was the station master, and both of them were determined that, at the very least, a full apology must be extracted from the young man. To begin with, it was explained to Wells that, should he show any sign of contrition, the whole matter would be forgotten. If he should choose not to apologize, he would be faced with a fine or dismissal. To help him reach a decision, Wells was permitted ten minutes to think it over.

In the circumstances it was a very generous offer, but Wells was in no mood to accept the proffered olive branch. Having stormed out of the office, he spent some of those minutes in conversation with John Golding, a station porter who asked about the outcome of the interview. Referring to the possibility of being dismissed, Wells concluded the conversation with the ominous statement that, if he had to leave, 'The old bugger would know about it.'

Returning to the office sometime later, Wells did not offer an apology. Instead, he maintained an aggressive and surly manner, refusing to listen to reason. Upon his leaving the station office, Henry Cox was left with little alternative other than to impose some form of punishment. It was whilst Cox and Walshe were discussing the matter that Wells re-appeared.

Pushing the door forward, he stepped into the office. In his hand was the fowling-piece, raised and ready to fire. Walking towards the station master, he proceeded to put those earlier threats into practice. In the sensationalized words of the most popular of the police sheets, Wells, having entered the office 'noiselessly', '... at the distance of a few feet fired point blank at his victim, and blew out his brains, shattering the head in a fearful manner.' (*Illustrated Police News*, 1 August 1868)

Following the shooting Wells made no real effort to escape, merely running across the station and clambering into a second-class railway compartment. It was here that he was discovered about twenty minutes later, when he was arrested and handcuffed by officers of the Dover constabulary.

At the subsequent trial, which was held at the Maidstone Summer Assizes, the only defence offered was the effect of those injuries suffered during the previous summer. According to his barrister, they had somehow influenced his mind. In the event, neither judge nor jury took much notice of this plea, with the jury returning a verdict of 'wilful murder' after having retired for only five minutes.

Mr Justice Willis, with the black cap resting on his wig, prefixed the passing of the death penalty with a few carefully chosen words: 'Thomas Wells, you have been convicted on the clearest evidence of a terrible murder, committed under the circumstances of atrocity so great as to be almost incredible. You have been rightly convicted; no one can entertain the slightest doubt. I would warn you to give up all hopes of this world and turn with bitter repentance to a God of mercy, in whose sight the best of us are nothing and whom the worst need not despair.'

Wells had become a major attraction in the police sheets that had once procured so much of his attention. As previously indicated, it was not the murder that had become the major talking point but the fact that his sentence had coincided with the abolition of public executions.

Having been sentenced in the Maidstone Court House, he was quickly taken to the nearby county prison where he was ushered into one of the cells set aside for the condemned. The prison authorities were giving much thought to the new Act, emphasis being placed on the need to find a new location for the gallows which then stood in a permanently erected position immediately next to the porter's lodge at the main entrance to the prison.

Digressing slightly, it is worth recording that public executions, prior to the new act, had been carried out in the Maidstone area from time immemorial, with Penenden Heath once the designated location. From the prison at Maidstone, those to be executed were often conveyed to Penenden Heath in batches, each securely manacled and guarded by armed warders. No sympathy was shown to the condemned in those earlier days, a seventeenth-century document recording that they were given only bread and water and allowed no visitors other than the gaoler, chaplain or surgeon.

From the prisoner's point of view, one of the worst aspects of a seventeenth-century-style execution was the final sermon given by the prison chaplain. In 1655 Freeman Sondes, condemned to death for murdering his brother, had to stand in front of the gallows for no less than thirty minutes whilst his many wrongs were listed by a zealous member of the clergy. Even then he was not put out of his misery, further time being set aside for prayers.

The final execution on Penenden Heath took place in December 1830, after which a new set of gallows was established on the site from which they now had to be removed. During the thirty-eight years leading up to the new Act, the citizens of Maidstone had the opportunity of witnessing a further twenty-eight executions, of which two involved the hanging of women.

The re-positioning of the gallows within the prison was not as easy as it might at first be thought. Not only had they to be brought inside the prison, but they had to be sited where they could be seen neither from the prison cells nor from a number of nearby houses that overlooked the prison. Eventually a former timberyard was considered to be the most appropriate area, it having the additional advantage of its own high wall. To make absolutely sure that the gallows would not be seen, an iron roof was constructed over one part of the yard, with the gallows placed underneath. Once it was in position, a cavity had to be dug into the floor, designed to receive the falling body.

As for Thomas Wells, he spent his last few weeks of earthly life occupied in writing letters, reading and giving attention to the ministrations of Sugden Frazer, the prison chaplain. Amongst those who received letters from Wells at this time were Henry Cox and the bereaved widow of Edward Walshe. In these letters he sought forgiveness, recognizing that he had committed a great wrong. A further series of letters was written to the girl he had once hoped to marry. Again, he expressed his sorrow, hoping that they might one day meet in heaven.

The execution took place on Thursday 13 August 1868, with William Calcroft the appointed executioner and George Smith acting as his assistant. Arriving from London at about nine o'clock on the morning of the hanging, they first took a drink at the New Inn (later the Wig and Gown) which stood opposite the courthouse. After a few minutes they crossed to the prison, pushing through a small crowd gathered outside the entrance.

For Wells, the appointment of Calcroft as his executioner was to prove most unfortunate. Despite having acted as public executioner for almost forty years, he was not particularly good at the job, being famous for a series of bungled hangings. Many of these failures had resulted from his persistent use of a short drop from the scaffold, which frequently resulted in the condemned man or woman's slowly choking to death. Far more humane was a longer, six-foot drop that ensured sufficient momentum for the breaking of the neck.

Despite the forthcoming execution being the first private hanging, the recently passed Act did allow the High Sheriff of the county the discretion of inviting members of the press. For this reason, sixteen journalists were present, as was the High Sheriff himself. In fact, the Act had made this particular dignitary in each county responsible for the overseeing of executions and, as a result, it was mandatory for him to be present.

One group of journalists specifically excluded from this first private execution were any who were connected with the police sheets, as an indication of official disapproval. These publications had to rely upon culling details from those papers whose representatives were present.

This did not prevent the *Illustrated Police News*

dispatching a reporter to view events from outside the prison: 'There were few, if any, strangers in the vicinity of the prison, and the town presented its ordinary appearance. A few of the tradesmen and other inhabitants might have been observed conversing together upon the sad spectacle that was going on within the walls of the prison, but the town generally presented a naked and extraordinary contrast to that which it has exhibited when executions have taken place in public.' (*Illustrated Police News*, 15 August 1868)

Inside the prison, the reporters from the more respectable newspapers were in a position to give free rein to their descriptive powers. A number concentrated on the style and dress of the two individuals engaged to carry out the execution. It was noted that the bearded Calcroft was wearing the same greasy suit and buttonhole flower that he had worn in those earlier public executions. Smith, 'a tall thin wiry man, with a keen eye, with his cheeks and part of his forehead partly shaved', was described as wearing 'a velveteen shooting coat, loose trousers, and a billycock hat, and looking like an acrobat who had donned his private clothes over his professional costume'.

As for a description of the execution, the failure of the *Illustrated Police News* to have a journalist present does not appear to have created any undue problems for this particular newspaper. Rather than invent an account, which would not have been that difficult, the editor simply chose to 'lift', without any form of acknowledgement, the exact words used in one of the local Kentish newspapers whose journalist was present: 'The culprit prayed fervently with the Rev. Mr Frazer, the chaplain, for a few seconds, and as the drop fell he was singing in a loud voice the 486th hymn. He appeared to die after two or three convulsive struggles.' (*Dover Express*, 14 August 1868; *Illustrated Police News*, 15 August 1868)

Despite the seeming suggestion of a fairly

instantaneous death, the reference to 'two or three convulsive struggles' was really indicative of Calcroft's inability to perform his job. With a longer drop there would have been no struggle. Reading between the lines, it is clear that Thomas Wells died in agony, remaining alive for some three or four minutes after Calcroft had released the drop.

Apart from requiring private executions, the 1868 Capital Punishment Amendment Act also introduced into the system a number of features that were to become all too familiar in future years. Amongst these was the posting of a notice of execution on the gates of the prison. At Maidstone, on that thirteenth day of August, it simply stated:

> We, the undersigned, hereby declare that judgement of death was this day executed upon Thomas Wells in Maidstone Gaol, in our presence.
>
> S. Musgrove Hilton, Sheriff of Kent
> C.W. Bannister, Gaoler of the Kent County Prison at Maidstone
> W.F.C.S. Frazer, Chaplain

A further provision of the Act was the necessity of an inquest in order to avoid any possible suggestion of the sentence's being carried out unfairly. That procedure was performed the same afternoon, the jury consisting of twelve tradesmen. Only a few witnesses were called, these giving evidence as to the identity of the body and of the court's sentence. It was, of course, very much a formality, with the jury soon retiring and subsequently returning a verdict of execution according to law.

So ended the life of Thomas Wells. That same week he was featured on the front page of the *Illustrated Police News*. Its pictures, mainly fanciful, showed him standing before the noose, his hands clasped in prayer, together with a series of smaller images that showed his last moments with the girl he had planned to marry, the posting of the sentence and the final burial.

Maybe these pictures, and the details concerning Wells, were responsible for turning the minds of others. It was always possible. But such a remark must remain unsubstantiated. All that can be said is that Thomas Wells and other readers of the police sheet were responsible for occasional irrational acts. Were they prompted by the papers they read or would they have carried out these same acts if they had never been exposed to these products of sensational journalism? It was a question the Victorians were never able to answer any better than modern sociologists.

– 3 –
The Fate of Sodom and Gomorrah, Biddenden, 1899

One of the most unusual murders to occur in the county of Kent took place in the tiny village of Biddenden during the winter of 1899. On this occasion not only was the murderer a woman but she was also the daughter of the local rector. Even more fascinating, however, is that Bertha Peterson, the murderer, in carrying out her gruesome task, chose to make no secret of the matter. In fact, she invited a number of unsuspecting acquaintances to witness the hideous act.

To throw some light on this strange affair, it is necessary to slip back to the year 1897. A memorable year for the entire nation, it saw Queen Victoria celebrating her Diamond Jubilee. Throughout the land, thousands of towns and villages chose a variety of ways to mark the event. Biddenden, of course, was no exception, planning a special children's party and village sports day.

Amongst those who helped organize some of these jubilee celebrations was John Whibley – the future victim of what became known as 'the Biddenden tragedy'. Mild-mannered and softly spoken, he was a popular member of the local community. He was tall and handsome, and his long, narrow face had a carefully trimmed brush moustache. If truth were known, this gave him an appearance somewhat akin to that of the stereotyped village Romeo.

Living in a traditionally styled Tudor town house in the High Street, Whibley used one of several spacious rooms to carry out the family trade of bootmaker. Apart from this, he had also acquired a number of additional jobs that included the position of Sunday school teacher, insurance agent and village correspondent for the popular local newspaper the *South Eastern Gazette*. It was, in fact, Whibley's own description of how Biddenden celebrated Queen Victoria's jubilee that appeared in the 29 June edition of that newspaper. The style he used was both brief and to the point: 'The bells rang out merry peals in the early part of the morning. About 1.30p.m. a tree was planted on the village green by Mr W.B. Tylden-Pattenson. A tea was given to all the school children and each child was presented with a book. The aged people were also given a substantial tea, and a programme of sports was carried out.'

For John Whibley, that year of 1897 was to prove somewhat traumatic. In January rumours had started to circulate as to his having sexually assaulted May Vane, one of the young girls who attended his Sunday school classes. Amongst those who heard and believed this gossip was Bertha Peterson, a fellow Sunday school teacher who had long despised Whibley – for reasons that are difficult to fathom. On several occasions she had written him a number of cruel letters that accused him of various misdemeanours. The most vicious of these attacks upon his character was dispatched in March 1897 and concerned those awful rumours:

> Mr Whibley, I have learnt that you are generally thought to have committed an atrocious crime against God and against an innocent, defenceless member of Christ – a little girl. I will not tell you how I learnt this. It is not necessary to do so,

> seeing that everyone to whom I have applied for evidence to clear you is not only unable to give such evidence, but refers me to several more people who are unable to help my researches in your defence. You are a communicant and a Sunday School teacher, and I ask you in God's name two questions:
>
> 1. Are you innocent of this crime?
> 2. Can you tell me how I can clear you?
>
> I will spare neither time, thought nor money, and no exertion shall be too great for me, if you will tell me how to do it. I await your answer.
>
> Bertha S.H. Peterson.

Not surprisingly, John Whibley reacted immediately. Desperate in his denial of the charge and aware that circulation of these rumours was being fanned by Bertha Peterson's interest, he declared himself willing to take a solemn oath as to his innocence. This she had indicated to be a possible solution.

Having firmly ensnared Whibley, Bertha decided that, before he undertook the oath, he should first suffer the indignity of a mock trial. Inviting him to the rectory, she had one of the rooms set out as an imitation court, with herself as both judge and prosecutor. Also present on this occasion, helping in the cross-examination of Whibley, was Alice Gould, Bertha's closest friend. Between them, they repeatedly went over the matter of the supposed assault, frequently deviating into other aspects of his private life.

Despite their persistence, neither could get Whibley to admit any guilt, and they eventually allowed him to take the promised oath. At this point another woman was invited into the room, her role being to act as a third witness. This was the Peterson's household maid, Alice Cooper. Her presence would appear to have been deliberately planned to humiliate the village bootmaker further.

With the oath taken, it was soon clear that Bertha was still unconvinced of Whibley's innocence. For this reason she wrote to him again, this time demanding that he give up his Sunday school duties and cease taking communion in the parish church. When he refused, she unleashed a further series of letters, each of them directed to a number of Church dignitaries, including the Archbishop of Canterbury and the rural dean. The letters were more or less identical, accusing Whibley of having assaulted May Vane and demanding that he be dismissed from all work connected with the church.

Apart from an acknowledgement, no one in receipt of these letters appears to have taken notice of her demands, although, in the village of Biddenden, her activities must have created a good deal of ill-feeling. If nothing else, it was sufficient to force John Whibley to resign from his Sunday school post.

Village gossip automatically centred upon the supposed assault. Had he or had he not assaulted the young girl? No doubt, the entire village would have taken sides, with some giving support to the accusations and others defending him. A further group might well have questioned Bertha's motives. Within the village community she had never been completely accepted, a number having clashed with her on matters connected with church affairs. In particular, she was known to be rather vindictive against those who stood in her way.

So exactly who was Bertha Peterson? Already it has been noted that she was a Sunday school teacher and had the added status of being the daughter of the elderly village rector. Generally considered to be a good-looking woman, she was, at the time of the mock trial, in her fortieth year. Apart from that vindictive side to her character, Bertha's behaviour was inclined to be erratic, whilst her ability to judge situations was misguidedly rash and frequently ill-considered. According to her best friend, Alice Gould, she did not take things as other people did: she would magnify small things and minimize big things.

Despite the occasional suitor, Bertha Peterson had never married, choosing to devote her life to 'good works'. Her particular interest was the well-being of village children. To this end she had attempted to establish a White Cross League in the village (an organization which had strong links with the Church of England, encouraging moral reform and social purity), whilst she used her own money to ensure that a local orphaned child was given a good home.

It was her work with children that had first led to Bertha's acquaintance with Alice Gould. In fact, the two had known each other for about fourteen years, the friendship having developed from Alice's attendance, as an eleven-year-old, at the Sunday school class taken by Bertha. As the years went by, their early friendship matured, the two of them becoming quite inseparable.

Apart from her erratic behaviour, Bertha also provided the village of Biddenden with a further talking-point. It appears that she was sometimes in the habit of walking through the village in her night clothes. As she was a well-endowed woman, with a full cleavage, one can only imagine the various jokes and innuendoes that would have been swapped each evening in the three village pubs.

Certainly there was something peculiar about Bertha Peterson's character. In fact, she had never really been the same since the death of her mother some years earlier. Apparently Mrs Peterson, who was an epiletic, had fallen into a lighted fire one Sunday morning. Although rescued, she was terribly burned and died in agony only a few hours later.

Yet such a terrible mishap cannot really explain why Bertha had such an entrenched dislike of John Whibley.

The affair of May Vane was certainly not the cause, for Bertha had been writing some fairly nasty letters to Whibley for at least two years. In virtually each one of them she had demanded his resignation from Sunday school teaching. Some believed that it resulted from his greater popularity with the children, others that there was a darker motive.

One possibility that seems to fit all the known facts was that Bertha Peterson was a man-hater. From this point of view, John Whibley could have represented all men, acting as a funnel for this general hatred. Indeed, there is an outside chance that Bertha also had latent lesbian tendencies. Certainly she appeared to be happy only in the company of Alice Gould, the two being a great comfort to each other. In May 1895, as it happens, Alice had actually moved into the rectory, and they had been known to have slept with one another. Whilst there is no suggestion of a sexual relationship, it is clear that Bertha preferred the company of other women and had difficulties in forming any kind of relationship with a man.

During the months following the mock trial of 1897, the village of Biddenden got on with celebrating Queen Victoria's Diamond Jubilee. Apart from the sports day and village party that John Whibley mentioned in his short article in the *South Eastern Gazette*, villagers also made a number of collections for various charities.

Throughout that period Bertha continued to harbour a grievance against Whibley. In particular, she used her position at the rectory to make difficulties for the man she so despised. During that summer she was asked by the Ancient Order of Foresters if they might be allowed to make use of a field adjoining the rectory for the purpose of holding a fête. When she discovered that John Whibley was to act as fête secretary, she told another member of the committee that the Foresters '…cannot have it under any circumstances if he has anything to do with it'.

The local gardening society received a similar rebuke during the same year. Writing to Bertha on behalf of the committee, the secretary asked her if she would be giving her usual donation of 5 shillings for distribution in sewing-prizes. Bertha wrote back insisting that she first required a list of those who were members of the committee. The secretary duly sent her those names, and John Whibley was included. In an immediate reply, she made it quite clear that she could not send the money while 'such a man belonged to the society'.

Other events in that year were also to have an influence on Bertha. During the summer her father was taken seriously ill, collapsing before his congregation as he took the morning service. As he was totally incapacitated, his responsibilities in the parish were temporarily taken over by his curate, the Reverend W. Raven. This, in itself, created further difficulties. Bertha decided that she was not happy with the situation and would directly run parish affairs herself. Not surprisingly, throughout much of the rest of the year, there were several clashes of opinion in which the newly appointed curate-in-charge found himself at the receiving end of her venomous tongue.

As for her father, most people fondly imagined that he was being carefully looked after by his loving daughter. Unfortunately, this was far from the truth. If anything, he was totally neglected. Allowed only the use of a camp bed, he would be left unattended for hours on end. Occasionally, so it would appear, Bertha would deign to bring him a light snack or a cup of tea.

The Reverend Mr Peterson must have been close to death when he was eventually rescued from this plight. His two brothers, not wishing to confront Bertha, secretly removed him from the house whilst she was at church. According to the doctor who accompanied them, the room in which he was being kept was more like a prison cell, bare of all furniture and lacking carpets. Furthermore, it had an offensive smell and was quite unsuitable for a sick person. At the time he referred to Bertha as being 'mad as a hatter'. He was nearer the truth than people generally imagined.

It was shortly after the removal of her father, in November 1897, that both Bertha and Alice Gould left the parish of Biddenden and moved to the nearby village of Egerton. Here Bertha had taken a lease on Hillside Cottage. Located on the edge of a small rise that leads into the village of Egerton, the cottage provided a number of excellent views which took in a mixture of farmland and woods. It was one of these woods, the adjoining Johnson's Wood, which was to play a minor part in the events that led up to Whibley's murder.

Although the lease on Hillside Cottage was frequently renewed over the next two years, Bertha and Alice made a rather surprising move at the beginning of 1898. For reasons best known to themselves, they entered into domestic service, finding employment with the Reverend Mr Bulma, whose parish was in Hertfordshire. The arrangement was hardly destined to be a success, with the two of them remaining there for no more than a few months.

In May of that year, Bertha found alternative employment as a nurse in a charity institution at Duxhurst in Surrey. On this occasion, Alice did not join her, the younger woman finding private lodgings elsewhere. They nevertheless kept in contact, exchanging a number of letters. Those from Bertha always dwelt upon the importance of religion and usually addressed Alice as 'my own darling little one'. Part of one of these provides a useful demonstration of both the nature and style of language she was using at this time: 'We must have on the whole armour of God, including HC [Holy Communion] or an evil angel may swoop down on us. Suppose JW [John

Whibley] is a devil. Our Lord said Judas was, didn't he, my lamb?'

The charitable institution that had accepted Bertha as a nurse was the Lady Henry Somerset Industrial Farm Colony, an organization that specialized in helping female alcoholics. Her duties were to take charge of one of the farm cottages and see that none of the women came to any harm. Inhabitants of the neighbouring towns of Reigate and Redhill would frequently catch a glimpse of her driving the colony's donkey and chaise. In later months, when she gained a degree of notoriety as a result of the murder, the *Kentish Express* carried a description of her that was culled from the local townspeople: 'Tall of stature and of commanding presence hers was a personality to be remembered, and many will recall having seen her engaged in shopping at one end of the borough or the other.' Those interviewed by the *Kentish Express* also mentioned that she usually wore a pince-nez which, it was suggested, 'lent something of hauteur to her appearance'.

As with her earlier stint in Hertfordshire, Bertha was to remain at the Duxhurst Farm Colony for only a short period of time. In fact, within nine months of her appointment she had been dismissed, senior staff apparently concerned about her mental condition. One of the factors guiding them towards this belief was her openly stated view that a certain Biddenden resident, John Whibley, was the Devil reincarnate.

Although Bertha was patently unsuited to the task of looking after women with drink-related problems, her dismissal from the Lady Henry Somerset Colony was to prove disastrous for both herself and Whibley. With time on her hands, she was able to give thought as to how he might be punished. Unable to bring others round to her opinion, she concluded that personal action was the only remaining solution.

Perhaps the best insight into her way of thinking comes not from the purchase of a revolver, nor from the fact that she spent many hours in learning how to use the gun, but from a picture she acquired in January 1899, depicting Jesus in the role of the Good Shepherd. She informed the shopkeeper from whom it was purchased that it was to be presented to her local school. This, in fact, was not her real intention. Instead, she had decided that John Whibley, at the very moment of his death, should be looking upon this picture.

Although it is impossible to untangle the complexities of Bertha's thoughts at this point in time, it does seem that she now considered herself to be God's instrument in an act of divine retribution. Possibly she thought of herself as a female version of 'the Good Shepherd', ready to kill any predator who endangered her flock. Certainly, in murdering John Whibley, she had decided that all children throughout the world would be saved.

As for the weapon to be used in this act of retribution, Bertha purchased a six-chamber Colt from the London branch of the junior Army & Navy store on 19 January 1899; she also took possession of 109 bullets. That same day she returned to Egerton, where she took the revolver into Johnson's Wood to learn how to fire it. Over the next few days she became increasingly proficient as she repeatedly aimed and fired the gun at a small wooden target. It was later estimated that this target was riddled with a total of forty bullets all of them fired at close range.

Eventually satisfied that she would have little difficulty in killing her victim, Bertha transferred herself to Biddenden. As the rectory was no longer available, she took a single room at the Rose Inn, informing the licensee that she would be staying until the following Monday.

Over the next few days, she engaged herself in seeking out a number of former acquaintances. To all of them she insisted that the purpose of her unexpected return to the village was that of seeking a reconciliation. In particular, she wished to apologize to all those with whom she had previously quarrelled. It was generally noted that her manner was far more affable than ever before and was in marked contrast to her behaviour in that year of 1897.

Amongst those she made a point of visiting were the Reverend Walter Raven and his two churchwardens. On a number of occasions she had refused to listen to their opinions, overruling decisions that had nothing to do with her. Promising to turn over a new leaf, she invited all three to attend a small ceremony at the village school. It was her intention, so she indicated, to give a picture of 'the Good Shepherd' to Mr Raven for passing on to the school's headmaster.

Henry Laverne, one of the two churchwardens, received his invitation when he met Bertha on one of the roads leading into the village.

'Good evening, Miss Peterson,' Laverne called out.

'Is that you, Mr Laverne?' asked Bertha. 'I was going to see you.'

Her manner, clearly friendly, left Laverne uncertain as to her motives. He had cause to remember her fiery temper two years earlier. Nevertheless, he shook her proffered hand.

'I am very pleased you meet me in the way which you have,' Bertha continued.

'I don't see any reason why I should not,' choosing to play down those earlier clashes. 'I can always go more than half way to meet anyone towards reconciliation.'

'Yes, and that is what I have come here for,' she continued. 'I have come here to put the wrong right.'

'I am very pleased to hear you say so.'

'Shall you be in church next Sunday morning?' she asked.

'Probably, unless anything unforeseen occurs.'

'I want you to meet me in the school room with Miss

Thirkell, Mr Pinyon, Mr Raven and Mr Whibley. I want to see you together to express my regret in front of you all to Mr Whibley for what I said about him and the way in which I have acted.'

During this conversation, in which she mentioned Miss Thirkell, a friend of hers, and Mr Pinyon, the other churchwarden, she also referred to the picture which was to be donated to the school. Finally, having outlined her intentions, she again hoped he would be present.

'You will come, won't you?' she asked.

Characteristically, John Whibley's invitation came in the form of a letter, which he received on the Saturday morning. Again, Bertha indicated that it was her intention to use the meeting as a means of apologizing for her earlier accusation:

> Dear Mr Whibley, I have had very much on my mind what took place between you and me in the Spring of '97. Are you willing to forget it? If so, what amends do you think you should ask of me? I was wrong in the attitude I took. I believe you were very badly treated – In any case it was not for me to judge. Will you come into the infant schoolroom after church tomorrow morning and look at a picture I am giving to the schools and shake hands. I have asked Mr Raven, Mr Pinyon, Mr Laverne and Miss Thirkell to come, and they will then see that I retract what I said about you. I want to give £1 1s to the Foresters, or to something that you are interested in, and if you will take it and pass it on to the treasurer I shall understand that you are willing to forgive and forget – Yours truly,
>
> B.S.H. Peterson

Following that Sunday's morning service in the ancient village church, both would-be assailant and victim made their separate ways to the local infant school. Of the four others who had been invited, only the Reverend Mr Raven was in a position to attend.

The infant school classroom lay immediately over the road from the church and had already been prepared for the occasion. In particular, Bertha had made a point of positioning the picture so that it was clearly visible, whilst a shopping-basket containing envelopes had been placed on a suitable desk. Upon the arrival of John Whibley and the Reverend Walter Raven, Bertha sorted out one of the envelopes which was addressed to the curate. Then, turning to Whibley, she asked him to 'look well' on the picture that she claimed to be presenting to the school.

With both men suitably occupied, Bertha removed the loaded revolver that was hidden in her clothing. Unseen by either man, she placed it close to the bootmaker's ear and pulled the trigger. A loud report reverberated around the room, and Walter Raven looked up ashen-faced. The little children of the world had been saved!

Having shot John Whibley in this climax to her madness, Bertha Peterson remained quite calm. At the time, some newspapers suggested that she also intended shooting some of the other invited 'witnesses', these also being people she had fallen out with. Yet this is not supported by the evidence. Her hatred was seemingly reserved for one man. The others she did not construe as guilty of a crime as serious as that of which she accused John Whibley. If this had not been the situation, she would have raised the revolver against Mr Raven. Instead, she allowed him to make an unobstructed exit, knowing that he would immediately report the murder and have her arrested.

'She has shot John Whibley,' were Raven's first words on coming across the school's head, Alfred Houghton. As was the custom in those days, his house immediately adjoined the school building.

Houghton, accepting the statement without question,

entered the infant school classroom, where he came across Bertha. She was still clutching the instrument of divine retribution.

'You may have this now,' she calmly stated, offering Houghton the revolver.

'Oh Miss Peterson, whatever made you do this?' Houghton asked.

'I had to do it to protect little children,' was her reply. It is questionable as to whether he understood what she meant. Anyway, at that point he relieved her of the revolver, though clearly he had no idea what to do with it.

'You don't seem to understand it. Will you let me have it back and I will show you how to open and unload it?'

Houghton preferred to retain the gun, thinking that it would be best if he just held it in a downward position. Bertha, accepting that he was not going to return it, decided to walk into the village.

By now, a small crowd had begun to gather at the school gate, and it was a member of this assembled group who was to be finally responsible for apprehending Bertha. Unlike most murderers, she was not attempting to escape in the accepted sense of the word. She had no reason to. From her viewpoint, she had done nothing wrong. Her simple intention was to return to the Rose Inn, where, presumably, she had ordered lunch. What else was she to do on a Sunday afternoon?

The man detailed to bring her back was Nasey Avery, a harnessmaker who lived next door to the school. Having heard raised voices, he had come over to the school gate and been told of the shooting. Houghton, upon seeing the face of a trusted neighbour, asked him to stop Bertha Peterson going into the village. Rushing after her, Avery found her reluctant to accompany him.

'You will have to come,' Avery ordered.

'I suppose, Mr Avery, you know what I did this for?' she asked.

'No, Miss Peterson, I do not,' although he could probably guess. But her continued declarations must have done nothing more than confuse the poor man.

'I did it in self-defence.' she claimed. 'I suppose you know that a woman is justified in killing a man! But a child is not able. I did this to protect little children.'

Upon bringing her back to the school, Avery also had the presence of mind to send two young boys to go and get the village constable, Alfred Mungham. Unlike Cobham's village constable of 1843, Mungham was no amateur, being a member of the County Constabulary that had been formed forty-one years earlier. Trained in basic detection, he was not going to make the same mistakes as the bumbling Dawes. On his arrival, he made it clear that no one was to enter the building, going on to inform Bertha Peterson that she would be placed under arrest.

'Very well,' was her only reply.

After he had given her the legally required caution, she was taken to the Chequers Inn for safe-keeping. Whilst awaiting the arrival of other officers, she engaged Mungham in conversation.

'Are you married?' was her first seemingly aimless question.

'Yes,' came the reply.

'You have no children, I suppose?' However, before he could answer this second question, Bertha chose to continue. 'I had to do this.'

Later she was to make a general accusation against the police. Still talking to PC Mungham, she asked, 'Where have you gentlemen been to allow this man to outrage little children?'

Mungham's reply goes unrecorded.

For the police sheets and the 'penny dreadfuls' the 'Biddenden Tragedy', as it was known, became a temporary *cause célèbre*. It contained all the ingredients upon which these papers survived. Making much of Bertha's fine physique, the *Illustrated Police Budget*, a true product of the gutter press, carried a variety of drawings that included several views of Biddenden school and other scenes connected with the murder. One, in particular, attempted to show Bertha Peterson at target practice in Johnson's Wood. The outcome was a woman whose breasts had increased by the same number of inches as the years which had clearly been removed from her forty-two-year-old face. But this was the treatment that appears to have been given to all women who found their way onto its numerous drama-filled pages. It seems, from Bertha's point of view, that although she had tried to save young girls, the 'penny dreadfuls' had merely used her as a means of exciting the passions of their male readership.

Of course, Bertha Peterson was quite mad. She genuinely believed that what she was doing was correct. In fact, only recently she had written to another of her friends, a Miss Oliver of Canterbury, telling her of her belief that 'the fate of Sodom and Gomorrah' was hanging over Biddenden for allowing such a crime to go unpunished. To her former employer, Sister Eleanor of the Lady Henry Somerset Homes, she wrote another of her many letters, this time expressing the thoughts that were running through her mind after the murder had been committed. It was written from a remand cell in Maidstone Prison: 'I suppose it was my own fault, but you must understand that if I pretend now that I was not responsible for what I did on Sunday, February 5th, things will be worse than before for little girls and anyone who helps to make me out insane is very cruel to little girls. The men would make a good excuse of that, and it would be worse for little girls.'

The trial of Bertha Peterson took place in July 1899, when she was brought before the Assize court at Maidstone. The charge was 'wilful murder'. Amongst the newspapers represented at the trial was the *Illustrated Police News*, its journalist clearly trained in the art of producing a dramatic account that would hold the attention of any reader: 'The prisoner entered the dock with composure, took a look round the court, listened earnestly to the charge and pleaded guilty in a low tone.'

This plea of guilty made the task of the prosecution particularly easy, especially as they were also able to call such a reliable witness as the Reverend Walter Raven. Much of the trial, however, revolved around the general belief that Bertha Peterson was insane. The result was that the proceedings hinged less on the action of the day than on her past behaviour. A number of Biddenden villagers were called to the witness-box, all confirming her outrageous behaviour of 1897. To provide further support for her being insane, Dr Davis, Superintendent of the Kent County Asylum, was also called to the trial. He expressed his opinion that both before and after the murder Bertha Peterson had been suffering from strong delusions.

With all this placed before them, the jury had little alternative other than that of passing a 'guilty but insane' verdict. The judge concurred, sentencing her to be detained at 'Her Majesty's pleasure' Bertha Peterson was subsequently taken to the Broadmoor Criminal Asylum, where she spent the rest of her life.

– 4 –
Evidence of Guilt, Deptford, 1905

As the jury re-entered, a deep and meaningful silence immediately swamped the courtroom of the Old Bailey. After two hours of deliberation, the foreman was in a position to pronounce the findings of the jury. Were the brothers Albert and Alfred Stratton guilty of wilful murder? Had they entered an oil and paint shop in Deptford High Street and mercilessly beaten to death an ageing shopkeeper and his wife?

Hearing of this, one of the most hideous crimes of the early twentieth century, the entire nation had recoiled in shocked revulsion. Surely it was impossible for the British, who prided themselves on an ability to 'civilize' the rest of the world, to nurture and harbour two such evil men? Yet, even if the Strattons were innocent, the crime had still been committed. Someone had killed the couple, emptying a cashbox that contained no more than could be earned by any decent man in less than a month.

Maybe it was the tension of the moment. Throughout the previous two days the Strattons had remained totally unmoved. Scanning each jury member for signs of weakness, they had shown themselves both truculent and self-assured. But now things had changed. They were clearly nervous. Albert, the younger of the two, was pale and drawn, his hard-set face beginning to match his white silk scarf. Alfred, always the calmer, failed to control a sudden and convulsive smile. This was an outward sign of that increasing inner concern. Were they to be hanged?

As the air of expectancy reached new heights, the clerk of the court positioned himself before the jury. In carefully measured tones he addressed the foreman: 'Gentlemen of the jury, have you agreed upon your verdict?'

With the affirmative being given, the clerk continued, 'Do you find the prisoner Alfred Stratton guilty or not guilty?'

'Guilty,' came the reply.

Again he asked, 'Do you find Albert Ernest Stratton guilty or not guilty?'

'Guilty.'

Turning towards the dock, the clerk directed his attention to the horrified prisoners. 'Alfred Stratton, you stand convicted of wilful murder. Have you anything to say for yourself why the court should not give you judgment according to law?'

Receiving no reply, the clerk then addressed himself to Albert Stratton. Again, no reply was given. The prisoners were aware that only one sentence was possible.

It remained for the judge, Mr Justice Channel, to allow the customary black cap to be placed over his wig. The task before him was not one that he relished. With tears welling into his eyes, the judge turned towards the two prisoners. Choosing his words carefully, Mr Justice Channel reminded them of the terrible deed that had been committed.

'For that crime,' he declared, 'there is but one sentence. It is not my sentence. I have no option but to pass it upon you both.'

Around the court all eyes were trained upon the guilty pair. Everyone present was fully intent upon seeing how they would react. Many were to be disappointed. Instead of admitting their guilt in some way, the Strattons had re-discovered their earlier composure. Neither was to move a muscle.

'I implore you to make best use of what time remains to you in this world,' Mr Justice Channel continued, 'for I cannot hold out to you any hope that sentence for the crime in this case will not be carried out.'

The thoughts of the two brothers at this point in time are unknown. If they were ordinary human beings, despair, misery and sheer terror might have dominated their thinking. But these two callous individuals may have been above such emotions.

The judge continued with those final, chilling words: 'The sentence of this court upon you is that you be hanged by the neck until you are dead, and that it is further ordered that judgment be carried into execution in His Majesty's prison at Wandsworth.'

Upon this, the court chaplain, now standing before the judge, offered his solemn, 'Amen.' To this he added the words, 'May the Lord have mercy on your souls.'

In order to prevent any possible demonstration on the part of relatives or friends, the two brothers were quickly ushered down the adjoining stairs and into the cells below. Later that same evening they were taken to Wandsworth by horse-drawn prison van.

Outside the rapidly emptying courtroom sat a grieving mother. Having heard that both her sons had been removed to the condemned cell, she was in a terrible state. Whilst she had no sympathy with their crime, she was still their mother. Realizing she had now lost them for ever, the burden became too much. Shortly after Alfred and Albert had been whisked out of court, she collapsed under the strain. It was to be some time before she was in a position to be moved.

During the remaining days before the execution Albert

appeared to discover a personal solace in religion. Writing to his sister, he mentioned letters that had been sent to him by the prison chaplain and a former Sunday school teacher. 'They have been the means of my turning to Our Lord Jesus Christ, and have succeeded in diverting my course to hell and directing me to Heaven. The only way I have to repay them is to pray for them, not only here, but also in the other world which I am about to enter. I hope you pray for me, I am praying for all of you, and especially for Alfred.'

The elder brother, although in exactly the same predicament, was less taken with religion. Instead, he seemed more concerned with berating his mother for not having supplied the court with a piece of evidence he considered essential. It concerned an injury to his hand, a point which he raised in a letter written to her a week before the execution: 'I don't mind the turn events have taken in the least. I have asked to be allowed to see you, so I suppose it will be alright, if you come to visit us ... You all know the state my right hand was in, therefore you should have given evidence, but it is too late now. I don't know what they intend to do with my clothes and money – whether they will keep them or give them to you. The time passed very quickly at the trial, as it was the first one I had ever seen I was rather interested.'

Deptford, in those early years of the twentieth century, still retained a village-like atmosphere. Within many of its tightly packed houses were families whose connections with the area went back several generations. It was not unusual for aunts, uncles, cousins and grandparents all to be living in streets that were no more than a stone's throw from each other. Less welcome, perhaps, was the resulting lack of privacy, everyone knowing about everyone else's business.

For the working class in Deptford – and it must be

stressed that Deptford was a working-class community – there existed a great range of possible employers. Acting as a buffer zone between the borough and its river foreshore was a highly industrialized area made up of factories, various shipping wharves and a busy cattle market. The last served as both a major receiving port and a slaughter-house for foreign livestock destined for the London markets. Additionally, there was a regular cross-Thames ferry which allowed the possibility of employment in the Millwall Docks and Poplar ironworks.

Yet the one thing that could not be guaranteed was a permanent job. Many of those employers offered work on only a seasonal or casual basis. Frequent lay-offs resulted in high local unemployment and a constant fear of the work-house. It was this uncertainty that led many Deptford youths to join either the Army or the Navy.

Despite the close-knit nature of the Deptford community, there did exist one very strong dividing-line. Whilst many in the population supported themselves through honest hard work (when it was available), this did not apply to a small number of law-breakers. Of these, the vast majority were nothing more than petty criminals who resorted to the occasional act of theft in order to supplement a meagre wage or stave off hunger. At the local police courts, either Tower Bridge or Greenwich, the most commonly heard cases were those of minor assault, drunkenness and prostitution. For such crimes, the penalty was the choice of a small fine or a few days hard labour.

Proving somewhat more problematic was the existence of a hardened criminal element that based itself around the activities of the 'Muffler' brigade, a local street gang that had acquired an unwholesome reputation for violence and racketeering. The 'Mufflers', the name coming from the white collars they normally wore, came together during the evenings. First they would rendezvous at the pubs. In Deptford these rarely closed before midnight. Later they would move on to one of the many all-night 'coffee' stalls, which also served food and alcohol. These were notorious throughout London and metropolitan Kent, as they provided the Muffler Brigade and members of other street gangs with the chance to organize themselves. At these stalls, there was a great deal of gambling, fighting and general rowdiness. Occasionally this fixed routine would involve innocent outsiders. The 26 May 1905 edition of the *Kentish Mercury* told of an incident that involved one of its readers: 'A few months ago he and two other young men who were returning from a party stopped to patronise one of these stalls, and they had only been there a minute when a cup of coffee was poured over one of them, while another was pelted with eggs. Not the slightest offence had been given. Our correspondent remonstrated with one or two hulking ruffians and as a reward had his hat smashed and his coat torn.'

Amongst those who associated with the Muffler Brigade were Alfred and Albert Stratton. In some ways they were typical members of the gang. Both were in their early twenties – Alfred was twenty-two and Albert twenty, and neither could boast of having had recent employment. Slightly unusual for a member of the gang was the fact that Albert had seen a short period of service in the Royal Navy, discharged in 1904 for insubordination.

Of the two brothers, Alfred was very much the leader. A well-built, broad-shouldered individual, he described himself as a labourer. Few in the area could remember when he had last undertaken such work. Rarely, however, was he short of money.

One source of income that Alfred possessed came from gambling: he was prepared to bet on anything from boxing at the Whitechapel 'Wonderland' to the outcome of the Boat Race. A further source of income was derived from his relationship with Hannah Cromarty, one of the area's numerous prostitutes. On occasion, she was known to go out on the streets, and the pennies she brought home were used for such essentials as food and beer.

Hannah and Albert shared a single rented room at 23 Brookmill Road. They lived there for about six weeks, sharing the house with two other families. Also situated in this road was Carrington House, an apartment block that offered beds for the homeless. It was here that Albert Stratton sometimes took accommodation. This was a useful arrangement as it allowed the two brothers to remain in close contact. Furthermore, Brookmill Road, although technically in New Cross, was less than ten minutes walk from Deptford High Street and a certain paint and oil shop that had come to the attention of the Stratton brothers during the first few months of 1905.

Gambling and living off the proceeds of prostitution were not the only means by which Albert Stratton supported himself. Far more lucrative was a series of burglaries he carried out with Alfred. For such purposes, so the police later discovered, the two of them had a collection of specially shaped chisels and a number of face-masks that had been fashioned out of stockings.

The most damning evidence for these nocturnal forays was later to come from Kate Wade. Sometime towards the end of the previous December she had left her husband to live with Albert. The relationship had not worked out. Albert seems only to have used the unfortunate woman, living off the small amount of money she had saved. He was also two-timing her, having formed a separate relationship with a twenty-two-year-old domestic servant, Ellen Black.

From evidence that Kate later presented to the police, it appeared that Albert would frequently go out at night, returning with valuable ornaments she had not previously seen. She was also asked, on one occasion, for any of her old stockings. It is possible that Kate unwittingly helped dispose of some of these stolen items, but it was an accusation she bitterly denied when it was suggested by one of the Strattons at a police court hearing.

The crime for which Albert and Alfred Stratton paid the ultimate penalty took place early on the morning of Monday 27 March 1905. The original object was the theft not only of a cashbox but of its owners' life savings, which the Strattons, wrongly, supposed to be hidden on the premises. The shop, which specialized in house paint and related products, was one of several owned by George Chapman. The others were situated throughout metropolitan Kent, with a separate manager always appointed. At Deptford, this task had been given to Thomas Farrow, who lived over the premises with his sixty-three-year-old wife.

In the weeks leading up to the robbery the Strattons must have spent a good deal of time loitering in the High Street, keeping an eye on the various comings and goings. They would have noted that Thomas Farrow was an early riser. Frequently painters, on their way to work would knock at the front door, to be served well before normal opening-hours. Also, around 7a.m., Thomas Farrow would be seen on the front doorstep smoking a pipe. A more useful piece of information that the Strattons acquired from these vigils was that George Chapman would collect the previous week's takings on a Monday morning. It was this last factor that helped determine when the robbery would take place.

Over that preceding weekend, Alfred Stratton seems to have been in possession of little or no money. Sunday, for instance, saw neither himself nor Hannah able to afford an evening meal. For this reason, Hannah used her undoubted charms to acquire some ready cash. With Alfred out of the house, she brought a male customer back to the single room for a short liaison that resulted in her gaining a useful shilling. Whilst Alfred was more than aware of how Hannah earned her money, he seems to have viewed this particular sexual encounter with a good deal of suspicion. Upon his return and discovery of his semi-clad girlfriend with an unknown man, he reacted violently. Having thrown the man out of the house, he turned on her. Punching her to the floor, he kicked her several times in the chest before taking the shilling and once more going out.

Contrast this scene of hostility and degradation with the calmer and quieter evening spent by the Farrows. Thomas was not a violent or hate-ridden man, whilst his wife was a loving companion. Having used part of their hard-earned money on a small but sustaining meal, they spent some of the evening at the nearby Wesleyan chapel where they were regular attenders. In preparation for the busy week ahead, the elderly couple slipped into bed sometime around 9p.m.

Alfred and Hannah, on the other hand, did not repair their differences until midnight. With one of them having temporarily staved off the pangs of hunger and the other nursing a good many bruises, they called a temporary truce to their argument when they, too, gave way to the needs of sleep.

At approximately 1.30 that night they were woken by the sound of someone knocking on their front-facing window. Neither was particularly surprised when they discovered it was Albert. Apparently it was quite normal for the younger man to use this method of contacting his brother. That it was so late was the result of his having spent the last few hours in the company of Ellen Black.

The subsequent conversation between Albert and Alfred was conducted in hushed tones, but Hannah appears to have heard Alfred ask the question, 'Shall we do it tonight or leave it for another night?'

In desperate need of money himself and with this being a reference to the planned robbery. Albert seems to have given the affirmative. In any event, the two of them now decided to go out together, Alfred put on a dark blue suit, a pair of brown boots and a light checked cap. Albert was wearing an old brown suit, a bowler hat and the white collar that signified his connection with the Muffler Brigade.

It might seem strange that, for a robbery not to be carried out for a further six hours, the two brothers should leave quite so early. After all, the shop was no more than ten minutes walk from Brookmill Road. One explanation concerns the simple lack of an alarm clock. How would the Strattons, having planned to enter the shop around 7a.m., avoid oversleeping? Some of their neighbours relied upon Billy Gail to tap on their windows if they had to get up early. It is unlikely that the Strattons would have considered this a solution. Billy Gail was the local policeman!

A second reason for this all-night vigil was that they considered these hours to be the most sociable. Numerous street traders were to be found throughout the area and, assuming Alfred still had part of the shilling he had taken from Hannah, the Strattons could make purchases from either a 'hot potato can' or a whelk counter. Of even greater importance was the need to visit a coffee stall. The Strattons and other 'Mufflers' favoured one situated close to the Broadway music hall. Here they remained for a number of hours, setting up a card school and falling in with the ladies of the night. As the sun began to rise so did honest Deptford. Seeming to represent the very lifeblood of this multitudinous community, the appearance of daylight brought an ever-greater number of people onto the streets and byways. The High Street, in particular, became the centre of this renewed activity. Throughout its length and breadth tradesmen could be seen making their early morning deliveries. At the same time, determined-looking walkers began to surge towards Deptford station and the various tram stops on Evelyn Street and the Broadway.

Amidst this maelstrom of human activity the nocturnal

Strattons attempted to merge. It was just not their time of day. As with Transylvanian bats, the appearance of the sun threatened their equilibrium. Purposely moving forward, they made a beeline towards the High Street shop that proclaimed itself as George Chapman's oil and colour store. Gaily decorated, with seven other branches listed between two upper-storey windows, the façade included two mock Grecian urns that supposedly contained sample products of crystal oil and methylated spirits.

As the Stratton brothers approached, they almost certainly discovered Thomas Farrow, obligatory pipe in hand, sitting upon the narrow doorstep that faced onto the High Street. Certainly this was Farrow's regular morning practice and it seems unlikely that this particular March morning would be any different. What happened next must be pure guesswork. Presumably the Strattons approached unmasked. How could they wear the evidence of their intentions in a far-from-deserted main thoroughfare? Almost certainly Farrow recognized them, having frequently seen them in the area of the High Street. Could this be the reason he was murdered or did he choose to put up a fight?

All that is known for certain is that the Strattons left behind them a scene of bloody carnage. Thomas Farrow, beaten over the head with a jemmy, was left battered and bleeding and was to die within the hour. His wife, still in bed, must have heard the noise. Her only recourse was to scream. She was too old and frail to do anything else. To silence her, she was clubbed over the head with a blunt instrument. Rendered unconscious, she died three days later in the nearby Greenwich Seaman's Hospital. Having committed the deed, described as one of the foulest of the century, the two men emptied the cashbox of the week's takings. They were richer by a mere £9.

The evening newspapers were full of the crime. In

Deptford it was a main talking-point for the entire community. When the two victims were discovered, at around 8.30 that morning, an angry crowd gathered outside the shop. To help control the situation, local constables returning from night duty were informed that they would have to work a few extra hours.

In Brookmill Road to which Alfred returned sometime afer 9a.m., Hannah was in for a small surprise. Far from being short of money, her unpredictable companion appeared to have acquired a sudden windfall. Summoning a small boy who lived locally, Alfred gave the lad sufficient money to purchase some coal and wood. At the same time, he also sent out for some bread and bacon. To Hannah, all this was clearly very unusual, almost as strange as the distinct smell of paraffin that seemed to emanate from his clothing.

It was not until later in the morning that Hannah heard about the murder. Whilst the two of them were toasting bread in front of the newly made fire, they were joined by one of the women who lived in the same house. She was full of the news, having just returned from the High Street. Upon hearing of the attack, Hannah was clearly shocked. Alfred said nothing.

Later that afternoon, with a spare halfpenny Hannah purchased an evening paper. She wanted to read about the ghastly event that had taken place. Scanning the headlines that told of recent atrocities in the Russo-Japanese War, she turned quickly to the centre pages, where she came across a full description of what had occurred in Deptford High Street early that same morning. Bringing the paper home to show Alfred, she read out a description of two men whom a milkman had seen leaving the shop: 'The first was apparently aged between 25 and 30 and 5ft 6in to 5ft 7in in height. He had a round face, a rather dark moustache, and wore a blue serge jacket, the collar of which was turned up. It was, however, noticed by the milkman that he was wearing a white collar, and to this fact the police attached some importance to him being a member of the "muffler brigade". The man was also wearing a hard felt hat. The man's companion was about 24 or 25 years of age, 5ft 5in to 5ft 6in in height, hair light brown, and dressed in a rather shabby brown jacket suit, a grey cap and brown boots.'

Giving Alfred a contemptuous look, she simply asked, 'Isn't this description of one like you?'

'Do you think I could do a thing like that and walk about the streets afterwards?' came Alfred's unconvincing reply. Then, after a little more thought, he simply added, 'Think how well known I am.'

Hannah was far from satisfied. There were too many things that had gone unexplained. Apart from the smell of paraffin on his trousers, his shirt had also been torn. He had even asked Hannah to mend it, claiming it had happened during their argument the previous evening. For her part, she was certain that the tear had not happened then. Finally she remembered something else. Upon returning that morning, Albert had seemed strangely clean. Had he not been to the public baths close to the burgled shop? Why should he do this when they were so short of cash? And where had all that money come from?

Someone else who had read the description in the evening paper was Rose Wood, another of those who shared the same house. On the following morning she came upon Alfred adding some black polish to the brown boots he had worn on the morning of the murder. She offered to lend him some brown polish, but he made no reply. Taking a second look at the newspaper description, she later questioned him about the murder.

Indeed, she went one stage further. 'I know exactly who those two men are,' she told Alfred.

Again, no reply was offered. He had no intention of being drawn on the matter.

'In fact, I will not leave a stone unturned until I have brought the guilty one to justice,' Rose eventually declared.

Slowly the local community was bringing pressure to bear on the errant brothers, but it was neither of these two women who first reported their suspicions to the police. Instead, it was a certain Ellen Stanton. An employee of Crosse & Blackwell of Charing Cross Road, she had, on the morning of the murder, been on her way to Deptford station to catch her usual train. Crossing into the High Street, she had seen the two brothers, of whom she recognized only Alfred, running out of the High Street. At the time she had thought they had been running to catch a Broadway tram but then she saw them turn and run into nearby Wilson Street.

At first she thought nothing of the incident. She did not hear about the murder until much later that evening. Like the rest of Deptford, she was extremely shocked, having become accustomed to seeing Thomas Farrow on his doorstep each morning. When she did report the matter, the police acted almost immediately, carrying out inquiries. The decision to arrest the Strattons was given increased support when it was discovered that both had disappeared.

Nevertheless, it was felt certain that the two of them would easily be found on the Saturday. Both were keen attenders at football matches, with an important cup tie being played at Crystal Palace. Despite a large number of policemen being sent to the match, no arrest was made.

On the following day, the search was widened, policemen throughout the area being given the Strattons' description and told to arrest them on sight. This had its immediate reward, with Detective Sergeant Beavis coming across Alfred Stratton in the King of Prussia, one of Deptford's numerous pubs. Approaching the suspect, he informed Alfred that he was under arrest.

'Is it for living off women?' Alfred asked hopefully.

'No,' came the ominous reply.

'What then?'

'It's a very serious charge. I'm taking you to Blackheath police station.

'Tell me what for!' came the rattled response.

'Acting-Superintendent Kitch will tell you.'

As for Albert, he was arrested on the following day, still in the Deptford area. Detective Inspector Hailstone arrested him only a few hundred yards from the site of the murder.

The news of these arrests was of particular interest to the Fingerprint Branch of Scotland Yard. Formed in 1901, they had yet to play their part in the conviction of a murderer. In this case, however, one of their officers, Detective Inspector Charles Stockley Collins, had been successful in discovering a partial thumbprint on the inner tray of the Farrows' cashbox. As far as he could ascertain, it belonged to neither Mr or Mrs Farrow, nor to their junior assistant. An earlier hope that the thumbprint might lead to identifying the murderer proved false when 90,000 sets of prints already held by the branch failed to provide a possible candidate. However, when a print of Albert's thumb taken at Deptford police station on Monday 3 April was examined by the branch, Detective Inspector Collins positively identified it as identical to the one discovered on the cashbox.

The existence of this thumbprint as part of the accumulating evidence also played its part in undermining the confidence of the Stratton brothers. In their first appearance at the Greenwich police court, both showed little respect for the proceedings. The *Kentish Mercury* reported them as using the occasion to wave and smile at their friends, a few of whom were sitting in the public gallery. In a subsequent appearance, the following week, a first reference was made to the existence of a thumbprint on the Farrows' cashbox. To Albert this clearly came as a severe shock, so much so that, in the lunchtime recess, he came close to making a full confession. Calling out to William Gittens, the assistant gaoler at Tower Bridge police court, he asked, 'How do you think I'll get on?'

'I don't know,' replied the gaoler.

'Can Alfred hear?' the younger brother inquired.

'No, he's some way further along.'

'I reckon he'll be swung up,' continued Albert. 'I shall get about ten years.'

The gaoler, choosing to say nothing, was intrigued as to what his prisoner might be leading up to.

'He led me into this,' confessed Albert. 'Don't say anything to him, I shan't say anything until I can see he has got no chance and then ...'

Suddenly Albert broke off. All of a sudden he had realized what he was saying. To continue would be as good as suicide. His only chance was to keep quiet on the matter and stick to their rapidly crumbling alibi that they had both been asleep in Albert's room at the time of the murder. It was a fairly useless defence, but it was the only one they could devise.

'I don't want to be strung up,' was Albert's final plea to the gaoler. 'Alfred has never done any work in his life, only about a month.'

The trial at the old Bailey was to prove a *cause célèbre* for the Fingerprint Branch of Scotland Yard. Not only was it the first time they had become involved in a murder but the whole system of fingerprinting was brought under close scrutiny. In particular, the defence counsel tried to show that, despite some past successes with a number of minor crimes, it lacked reliability.

Amongst witnesses attacking the system was a certain Dr John Garston. Having taken the witness-stand, he proceeded to examine photographs of both Alfred Stratton's thumbprint, taken at Deptford police station, and the partial thumbprint found on the cashbox. Whilst the prosecution had claimed that there were eleven points of similarity (of which four would be sufficient), he claimed that no such similarities existed.

A gasp of amazement could be heard in the public gallery as Garston went on to claim, 'It is, of course, possible that they were made by the same individual, but not by the same finger.'

In effect, Dr Garston was attempting to undermine not only the whole of this investigation but the entire science of modern policing. If Inspector Collins, one of the most senior and experienced officers in the Fingerprint Branch, had got this basic fact wrong, the entire unit would have to be wound up. Furthermore, all those previously convicted by this system would demand that their cases be reviewed. Fortunately, the defence was ready for such an accusation, with the Crown prosecutor, Mr R.D. Muir, quickly producing the first of two letters that Garston had written. It was addressed to Mr Budden, solicitor for the defence: 'I am not quite sure whether the Treasury are going to call me. Should I not be called I shall be pleased to arrange with you to give expert evidence for the defence. It [the fingerprint system] is a splendid means of identification when properly used, but I have no hesitation in saying that the way it is being used by the police is that which will bring it in disrepute.'

Outwardly there was no problem with this particular letter. Dr Garston was an expert, having once been employed by the Home Office as an adviser on fingerprinting. However, on the formation of the Fingerprint Branch his services had no longer been required. This proved a source of grievance, and it was for this reason that he was now attempting to undermine these recent developments in forensic science. Yet, on the day Garston had written to Budden, he had also written a second letter. Also produced in court, it had been addressed to the Public Prosecutor: 'I would be glad to know whether you intend to call me as an expert in the trial of the Stratton brothers on the fingerprint impression which are to be brought forward, I understand, as evidence against them. I feel the Government has, perhaps, the first claim on my services. I may say that if I am not retained by the Treasury as an expert, I shall probably give evidence as such for the defence.' Clearly, this second letter was nothing more than an amateurish attempt at blackmail, Garston being desperate to be re-appointed to the post from which he had been dismissed.

Having read both letters to the court, Muir simply asked, 'How do you justify writing two such letters on the same day?'

'I am an independent witness,' came a rather lame reply.

Mr Justice Channel, raising his eyebrows at this point, chose to intervene. 'An absolutely untrustworthy one I should think, after writing such a letter.'

'I would have given the same evidence whether for the Treasury or the defence.'

'In neither of these letters do you say a word about wishing to see the impressions before giving evidence,' continued the judge. 'If you had, one could understand.'

Mr Justice Channel was extremely annoyed and did not want Garston influencing the jury in any way. For this reason he further intervened as Alfred's barrister attempted to repair some of the damage: 'Isn't there a limit to whitewashing this gentleman? It has done your client a lot of harm.'

Despite having taken against this particular witness, the judge was himself a little suspicious of fingerprints as evidence. In his summing-up to the jury, he told them that the fingermark on the cashbox '... was made only with perspiration and was not so satisfactory as it would have been if the material with which it was made had been of a kind that would give a better impression'. As a result, he felt that the jury should not 'act upon it alone'.

Following those directions and the judge's summing-up of the evidence, the jury retired. It is unimportant how the jury used the fingerprint evidence. Far more important is that it showed, beyond doubt, that the police had arrested at least one of the murderers and were then able to assemble a good deal of additional evidence. The county of Kent had rarely seen two such evil characters within its ancient boundaries.

– 5 –
In the Footsteps of George Joseph Smith,
Herne Bay, 1912

Next time you visit Herne Bay, one of Kent's quieter and more somnolent seaside resorts, why not try something different? Instead of relaxing on the occasionally sun-drenched beach or strolling along a more frequently wind-swept promenade, may I suggest you take a walk into the past? Accept this chapter as your guide and follow in the footsteps of George Joseph Smith, the most callous murderer ever to stand trial at the Old Bailey.

As with any guided tour, a brief introduction is clearly necessary. Before starting your tour, I would like you to know that Herne Bay is completely innocent of breeding this man and his insatiable desire to grow rich at any price. He was, in fact, a visitor to the town, arriving here during the summer of 1912. Already he had thoughts of committing murder, his intended victim being Bessie Mundy, a travelling-companion who believed herself to be his lawful wedded wife.

The reason for his choosing Herne Bay as the venue for this terrible deed is easy to fathom: he had never previously been within fifty miles of the town. This to him was important. He was a confidence trickster who preyed upon unattached women, and Herne Bay provided little risk of meeting one of his former victims and ending up in the police courts.

Of particular significance when discussing George Joseph Smith is the magnetic personality which he undoubtedly possessed. In fact, he had the ability not only of attracting women but of totally destroying their in-built defences. Furthermore, once his chosen victim had come within his grasp, she was incapable of denying him even the most outlandish of requests. These strange and terrifying qualities continued to attract women even after his various crimes were publicly known. At the committal proceedings held at the Bow Street police court following his arrest in 1915, large numbers of women were prepared to queue all night simply to get a glimpse of him. Others, upon entering the court, would deliberately sit as close to him as possible, prepared to touch any part of his anatomy that came within reach.

Needless to say, masculine society was not amused by these antics. All the journalists who covered the trial were genuinely shocked and failed to provide any reason for this behaviour. As for court officials, they attempted to prevent a repetition of these events once the trial had moved to the Old Bailey. In particular, efforts were made to reduce the number of women entering the court. Amongst those who did gain entry, however, were some of London's most exclusive prostitutes. It appears that they would often spend the entire day drooling over the man and discussing his various charms.

A simple description of Smith provides only a few possible clues as to why he was so attractive to women. It might have been the fact that he always chose to present a smart appearance, normally wearing an ageing black suit. As for his looks, there can be no doubt that Smith was both tall and dark, but he was not particularly handsome. Turning to another possible clue for the basis of this magnetism, we arrive at his eyes. Everyone who met him seems to agree that he did not just look at people but stared at them with unrivalled intensity. Some even suggest that these dark brown eyes were responsible for placing his victims into a permanent trance.

Financially, Smith relied entirely upon those various women he duped throughout the passing years. Deliberately seeking out unattached women, he would first gain their confidence and then relieve them of their life savings. Invariably, this sequence of events would begin at a seaside resort, experience having taught him that the women most susceptible to his charms were usually long-stay residents in one of the numerous guest houses that dominate these towns.

Judging by the experience of some of these victims, he always used the same line of approach. Having first identified his target, he would patiently wait for an appropriate moment. As a rule, this was when the unsuspecting woman was comfortably seated on the promenade or on a park bench. Sitting next to the chosen quarry, he would then engage her in conversation. Beginning with references to the weather, he would slowly become more daring, introducing a degree of flattery and the carefully placed remark that his new-found acquaintance had 'a fine figure'.

Amongst those who fell for this line of patter was Bessie Mundy. She was to prove the most forgiving of all his victims, prepared to offer him the chance of re-entering her life even though he had already stolen some of her savings. Smith was ready to throw caution to the wind and take up with a former victim because she still had an even greater sum of money that he later wished to acquire for his own purposes.

As for Bessie Mundy herself, she was quite simply one of those many lonely women upon whom Smith so frequently preyed. Despite her thirty-three years, she had either tactfully avoided the company of men or been unsuccessful in her attempts to find a companion. Certainly she was a very reticent individual, feeling both embarrassed and awkward in the company of men. In part, this resulted from the low esteem in which she held herself, having the belief that she was plain and unattractive. Certainly she was not blessed with an ideal figure, but careful dressing and the re-arrangement of her hair would have done much to mitigate her above-average height and exaggerated facial features.

George Joseph Smith and Bessie Mundy first met at Clifton during the early summer of 1910, with Smith introducing himself as Henry Williams. In the first few days of 'friendship', their conversations were dominated by idle chatter and a desire to pass the time of day. However, when Smith (alias Henry Williams) discovered that Bessie was the owner of a small fortune, he soon chose to alter the nature of their relationship. Declaring himself to be in love with the poor woman, he began to talk of marriage and of a future life together. In doing so, of course, he forgot to mention one small obstacle. Not only was he already married, but since that first marriage in 1899 he had bigamously married and left three other women.

Bessie, blinded by her own feelings of ecstasy, accepted all she was told without giving the matter any real thought. At last she had found a husband, a man who would care for her and remove her from the interminable guest houses that were her only home. As a result, she never once questioned her suitor's background, nor asked for proof of his bachelor status.

The marriage ceremony took place at the Weymouth registry office on 26 August. Smith made good use of the two weeks that followed. During that time he worked towards the goal of getting his hands upon part of her savings. Although he was aware that she had a total fortune of £2,500 (an amount that would now be worth

£250,000), he knew that this was tied-up in a trust fund controlled by her uncle and brother. Far more accessible was a smaller sum that had accumulated in the form of interest from the larger amount held in trust. Consisting of approximately £100 and also in the hands of her two elder relatives, it was hers to call upon as and when required.

Despite their surprise at the speed in which she had chosen to marry, both the trustees were happy to release the requested sum. When the cheque arrived, on 13 September, Smith demanded that it should be immediately cashed and the sum handed over to him for safe keeping. Bessie happily agreed to this request. It was the last she was to see of this portion of her savings.

Within minutes Smith told her that he had an important appointment and would meet her later. In fact, she was not to see him for two years. Upon her return to the guest house where they had been staying, she found a letter that attempted to explain why he had now left her. It contained a number of appalling accusations which the innocent and unworldly Bessie must have had a lot of difficulty in understanding. Its wording provides evidence as to how cold and pitiless the man could be:

> Dearest, I fear you have blighted all my bright hopes of a happy future. I have caught from you a disease which is called the bad disorder. For you to be in such a state proves you could not have kept yourself morally clean ... I don't wish to say you have had connections with another man and caught it from him. But it is either that or not keeping yourself clean. Now for the sake of my health and honour and yours too I must go to London and act entirely under the doctor's advice to get properly cured of this disease. It will cost me a great deal of money, because it might take years before I am cured. The best thing for you to tell the landlady and everyone else that I have gone to France on business.

Imagine the shock poor Bessie must have received on reading those lines. This man, this creature, was callous beyond dispute. Yet, despite such treatment, despite these accusations of her promiscuity and of her being riddled with disease, despite the fact that he had walked off with her money, she was still prepared to forgive. And that, quite frankly, is the most amazing thing about George Joseph Smith: women did let him walk all over them.

The chance to forgive her runaway 'husband' came in March 1912. Having by that time moved to Weston-Super-Mare, Bessie found her erstwhile lover waiting for her on the promenade. His return to the woman whom he claimed still to love was prompted by no other reason than the possibility of getting his hands upon her entire fortune.

As indicated, Bessie showed no ill-feelings towards the man, choosing to believe in a slightly altered version of events in which Smith now claimed that he had indeed, feared that he had contracted a disease but that he had left only so as to prevent Bessie catching it. As for the money he had taken, this he considered to have been nothing more than a loan which he would repay as soon as possible. To overcome any possible doubts, he immediately took Bessie to the office of a local solicitor and signed a promissory note in which he agreed to repay the 'loaned' money.

It was shortly after the reunion that Smith decided the two of them should live in Kent. It has already been explained why Herne Bay was chosen, but prior to their arrival here they did visit a few other towns. Entering the county via London, they spent a week or more at Woolwich, Smith having some business to transact with the local building society before they moved on to Ramsgate (Flora Road), Ashford (Beaver Road) and finally Herne Bay.

With these introductory remarks in mind let us now

begin that promised tour of Herne Bay, in the footsteps of Kent's most notorious murderer.

The starting-point is the town station, where the couple first arrived sometime during the middle of May 1912. Smith seemed to prefer travelling by train, although on this occasion he would have had a more difficult journey than was usually the case. Mainly this resulted from the lack of a direct line, with the two of them having to travel via either Faversham or Ramsgate. Either way, the journey was somewhat tedious.

From the station, they proceeded along Station Road, walking as far as the junction with King's Road. As they approached the junction, they got their first glimpse of the sea. Turning right, they then walked almost the full length of King's Road, eventually stopping at No. 4 Kingsbury Villas, where they agreed a rate for bed and breakfast.

Kingsbury Villas still exist, being located almost at the junction of King's Road and Canterbury Road. Part of a set of mid-terraced houses built in 1883, No. 4 has a single bay window that faces away from the sea. Although the particular room the couple were given cannot be verified, it may well have been the front-facing upper room, this being amongst the most spacious in the house.

Although it is not known exactly what the couple did over the next few days, they may have spent time savouring the delights of this popular pre-war resort. At the East Cliff Pavilion they could have passed a happy hour or more listening to the band of the 7th Lancers, whilst on the pier the 'Jollity Boys' would have entertained them with a mix of music, singing and comedy. If, on the other hand, moving pictures were to their taste, there was always the 'Cinema de Luxe' which once stood at the western end of the High Street. The film being shown on the week of their arrival was *The End of Robespierre*.

If the couple did choose the 'Cinema de Luxe' during

that particular week, Smith would have been reminded of that famous incident in which Charlotte Corday killed Marat whilst he was in his bath. Is it not possible, therefore, that George Joseph Smith, otherwise known as 'The Brides in the Bath Murderer', first acquired the essence of an idea that was to come to fruition just two months later?

In between these lighter moments, Smith was also concentrating upon the need to acquire more permanent accommodation. To remain with him, we follow him as he made his way to Victoria Park, which was then considered to be a rather superior residential quarter. It was not that Smith intended to move into this road. Instead, he wished to meet a certain Frederick Henri Wilbee whose home and business address was Grosvenor House. Situated in Victoria Park and currently owned by Kent County Council, it is a large nineteenth-century town house that can be found on the north side of the road. Smith's object in visiting Wilbee was to arrange a lease on a small High Street house that was currently vacant.

Upon his reaching Grosvenor House, the door was opened by Wilbee's middle-aged secretary, Carrie Rapley, with whom all transactions had to be carried out. Shown into the front room, where Carrie had her office, Smith was now confronted by one of the few women who was eventually to suspect and then take a dislike to him. However, Carrie's attitude during that first meeting was far from antagonistic. Indeed, on this occasion she went out of her way to help Smith, ignoring a number of problems that would normally have resulted in her refusal to allow a prospective client to be given a lease. Perhaps the normally discerning and businesslike Carrie Rapley had also fallen under the man's influence.

With the initial formalities out of the way, Smith's first enquiry concerned the rent. Carrie, trying not to be too officious, gave him the necessary details. She started by saying that this particular house (No. 80 The High Street) would have to be let at a rent of £18 a year, payable in advance.

'Will that suit you, Mr Williams?'

'Ah! The money's no problem, but I am afraid it could not all be paid in advance.

'Well, if it's only a question of the payments, I'm sure we can arrange something to suit you. Will a monthly payment be in order? Naturally you'd still have to pay the first month in advance.'

Having indicated this to be satisfactory, Smith then perused the printed form of agreement. In the meantime, Carrie went on to ask him how many would be occupying the house.

'Only my wife and I. We have been married two years – no family.'

'Before we go ahead with this agreement, Mr Williams, can you supply a reference?'

'Unfortunately, no,' Smith replied. 'But I can assure you that my wife and I are totally trustworthy. Do you wish to speak to her?'

'No, that will be quite unnecessary,' declared Carrie, although she was aware that no previous tenant had failed to supply any form of reference. 'But surely your previous landlord can supply a reference?'

'Never had one,' Smith lied.

'Oh, so where have you been living for the two years of your marriage?'

'We have been going about to different places and living in furnished rooms,' he continued to lie. 'We have just come from Ashley.'

'Can you give me a solicitor's reference?'

'No, I haven't got a solicitor either.'

'Have you a banking account?' she persisted.

On that he put his hand in his pocket and pulled out a

book. Carrie looked at the cover and said with surprise, 'Oh, that is a post office savings book. I do not mean that sort.'

She held out her hand to take it, but he put it back again, declaring, 'You need not be afraid. There is between 50 and 60 pounds there.'

'If you are going to furnish the house, it won't leave much to live on,' she pointed out.

'My wife has a private income paid monthly. I have not got anything except that; I dabble in antiques. As for my wife, I might just as well tell you she is a notch above me. She is the daughter of a bank manager, and I met her in a boarding house. Her friends did not all approve of the marriage.'

With anyone else, Carrie would have been completely exasperated. She was quite used to refusing people her employer's accommodation. But with Henry Williams something had got the better of her. Despite his lack of references and inability or unwillingness to prove his financial status, she decided to let him have the house. For her own security, however, she decided she ought to mention the matter to her boss. This she briefly did, quickly returning to Mr Williams. Everything was soon settled, with it being agreed that he should have an annual lease, paying the rent on a monthly basis. The house was fit for immediate possession.

Before leaving Victoria Park, it might be of interest to take a look at one other house in this road. Situated on the corner with Bank Street and built in the same year as Kingsbury Villas, there exists a smart two-storey residence known as Silverdale. Also, at one time, owned by Henri Wilbee, it was, in that year of 1912, the home of Carrie Rapley. As she had been in Wilbee's employ for over thirty years, it is possible that she had some say in its design. This might well explain the imaginative use of verandas, a building style that is sadly lacking in most of the other houses that it seems likely Wilbee was responsible for building.

Continuing to follow in the footsteps of George Joseph Smith, the next point to aim for is the High Street and a shop that carries the number 159. Having a distinctive 1930s appearance, this building stands on the same site as the house which Smith had agreed to rent. That it has a totally different number merely results from a re-numbering of the entire High Street at a later date.

In 1912, if you had been standing on this same stretch of the High Street, you would have been looking at a fairly ordinary collection of two-storey mid-Victorian houses that were not dissimilar in style to the group that made up Kingsbury Villas. The house that Smith had agreed to rent had three rooms on the ground floor, made up of a kitchen, dining-room and living-room, whilst upstairs there were three bedrooms. From this brief description it will be noted that the house lacked a bathroom, whilst any water had to be heated on a gas stove in the kitchen.

Now, in choosing to lease this house, Smith had but one object in view. He simply wished to ensure that Bessie was totally convinced as to his sincerity about their future life together. Only by agreeing to this long-term lease, together with the purchase of furniture, did he feel that Bessie would be satisfied. Having gone through this ritual, however, he then felt safe to broach the matter of the money held in trust. To Bessie, he now suggested that the trust fund should be somehow dissolved so that the money could be used for the purpose of setting him up in the business of selling antiques.

Again, however, all this was no more than a cover. Smith did not really believe that the money would be released, especially as both trustees were aware that Bessie was once more in his clutches. Instead, it permitted him to introduce a second and far more important idea. If, as he was now suggesting, the two of them should set up in business, it would also be a good idea if they made mutual wills that named each other as beneficiaries.

It is at this point that we confront the real reason for Smith's re-entering Bessie's life. Having doubtless taken legal advice, he was aware that the trustees could never be made to dissolve the trusteeship whilst Bessie was still alive. On the other hand, should she die, the terms of any will would take immediate effect. In other words, if she named her 'husband' as the sole beneficiary of all her wealth, Smith, under the name Henry Williams, would acquire the £2,500 that had eluded him two years earlier.

To advise further on these matters, Smith insisted that they should approach yet one more solicitor, this time choosing a certain Philip de Vere Annesley. His former offices, also situated in the High Street, are fairly easy to locate, being above Lloyd's Bank and on the corner of William Street. When the couple entered Annesley's office sometime on 18 June, the two sets of wills, one of them already signed by Bessie, were handed over to Annesley so that he might confirm their validity.

'These, I am afraid, are out of order,' was the solicitor's first comment.

'How do you mean?' asked Smith.

'Well, for a start, they are not witnessed!'

This did not appear to worry Smith a great deal, and he seemed quite happy for the solicitor to take charge of the affair. At that point, the matter of the trusteeship was also mentioned, with Annesley eventually confirming that the trust could be dissolved only if both trustees agreed. In fact, it was Annesley's final confirmation of the impossibility of ending the trust, together with the witnessing of a further set of wills, that sealed the fate of Bessie Mundy. From that point onwards, Smith chose to finalize a series of plans that would soon result in the death of the woman he claimed to love.

The idea of drowning Bessie in a bath was certainly a

stroke of genius. Whether he had practised it elsewhere or was prompted by the Robespierre film will never be known. Whatever the truth, Smith had hit upon a seemingly infallible solution to his small problem. It simply required Bessie, in the presence of her 'husband', to settle herself into a moderately filled bath. Smith would then move himself to the foot of the bath, where he would make a sudden grab for her legs. As he pushed them upwards, her terrified face would slip below the surface, and within thirty seconds she would be dead. As a courtroom experiment later showed, it was a horrifyingly easy way to kill someone, with the victim powerless to save herself even when aware of what was intended.

One immediate problem that confronted Smith during this period of planning was the lack of a bath in the newly acquired High Street house. Indeed, his failure to ensure that such an item was part of the house probably suggests that the idea of using a bath as an instrument for murder had only recently claimed his attention.

For those choosing to follow in his footsteps, it is interesting to note that the bath eventually used was purchased from Adolphus Hill, an ironmonger whose shop was situated on the corner of William and Mortimer Streets. This shop, as it happens, is still there, having long since gone over to the sale of vegetables. The bath, which was apparently delivered on 9 July, was of a standard sloping design, being five feet in length and free standing. The cost of this addition to the Williams household would have been 37s. 6d, but it was a sum that Smith never bothered to pay. Having used the bath to kill his wife, he merely returned it to the shop from whence it had been acquired. He was never one to waste money!

With the method of Bessie's demise now determined, Smith had to ensure that no one would suspect his involvement. It was for this reason that he made one more essential foray onto the crowded streets of this popular seaside town. Accompanied by Bessie, he made the short journey to Canterbury Road, where Dr Frank Austin French had a small surgery. Again, it is possible to follow in the murderer's footsteps, the particular surgery being attached to Hollamby House, a building that still stands and which is located close to where Canterbury Road intersects with the High Street.

Arriving at the surgery early on Wednesday 10 July, Smith informed the doctor that on the previous day Bessie had suffered a fit that had rendered her unconscious. For her part, Bessie seems to have said very little. What could she say? The fit to which her 'husband' referred was non-existent! Since the previous day he had been trying to convince her that a sudden stumble was really something far more serious. Perhaps she did not wish to annoy her husband, especially as he seemed genuinely concerned. For this, or some other reason, she seems to have gone along with the story. Indeed, if the truth were really known, probably she was rather flattered by all this attention. As for Dr French, one of the youngest and least experienced of Herne Bay doctors, he was certainly convinced and prepared to offer his patient a sedative in the form of bromide of potassium.

The object of this little visit was simply for Smith to gain evidence that his 'wife' was subject to fits. If other people were convinced of this, especially if those others included a doctor, her subsequent drowning would be that much more believable.

To give further support to the idea of Bessie's being subject to fits, the assistance of Dr French was to be utilized on one more occasion. This time it was in the form of an emergency, with the doctor being called out at 1.30a.m. on the following Friday. According to Smith, who fetched the doctor, his 'wife' had suffered another loss of consciousness. Upon his arrival at their house just a few minutes later, he found Bessie sitting up in bed. According to a statement made by the doctor during cross-examination at the Old Bailey trial: 'The best way I can describe her condition is that she was as some one who had been recently wakened from sleep on a hot night.'

And this is just what had happened. It was, in fact, one of the hottest nights of year, with Bessie, not surprisingly, saturated in a good deal of perspiration. Furthermore, her 'ever-loving husband' had suddenly woken her from a deep sleep, claiming that she was having another one of her fits. The doctor, upon examining her, found her pulse to be normal and showing no signs of that claimed loss of consciousness.

Possibly Bessie herself was now concerned as to the state of her health. Without being aware of it, she was being told that she had had a fit on two separate occasions. Her husband, still showing great concern, insisted that she tell one of her relatives. The result was that on the following day she put pen to paper, informing her uncle of this sudden down-turn in her health. It is likely that the precise wording of the letter was not hers but that of Smith. Certainly the exaggeration of the care she was being given would imply that he had some influence over the exact words used: 'Last night I had a bad fit, and once again on Thursday night. It has left me very weak and suffering from nerves and headache, and has evidently shaken my whole system. My husband has been extremely kind and done all he could for me. He has provided me with the attention of the best medical men here, who are constantly giving me medical treatment, and visiting me day and night. I do not like to worry you with this, but my husband has strictly advised me to let all my relatives know and tell them of my breakdown. I have made out my will and left all I have to my husband. That is only natural, as I love my husband.'

As for the act of murder that would make George Joseph Smith an extremely rich man, this took place early on Saturday 13 July 1912.

Filling the newly acquired bath from water previously heated in the kitchen, he insisted that his doting wife would feel much better after a good long soak. Accompanying her into an upstairs bedroom where the bath had been previously placed, he doubtless helped her undress.

As she stepped into the bath, Smith would probably have been callous enough to offer a few loving words. Perhaps his insatiable sexual appetite was excited by the prospect. Maybe they had only just made love. Following those whispered endearments, the unsuspecting Bessie settled into the water that had been so carefully brought from downstairs. As she closed her eyes, Smith slipped round to the foot of the bath. Clasping both her legs, he gave one sudden pull.

Bessie stood not a chance. Taken completely by surprise, she could only grab at a small piece of soap. It could not possibly have saved her. Indeed, it merely helped Smith in his later declarations that she must have suffered another fit. At the subsequent inquest, it was agreed that her grabbing the soap was proof of such a fit, it being assumed that a woman forcibly drowned would let go of the soap and seek something firmer by which to save herself. Later experts were to disagree.

Having carefully checked that Bessie was dead, it was now essential that Smith act like any other grief-stricken husband. To this end, Dr French was quickly informed of Bessie's death, receiving a simple hand-written note sometime after eight o'clock that same morning. As with nearly everything else written by Smith, it was terse and to the point: 'Can you come at once? I am afraid my wife is dead.'

Upon arriving at the house the doctor was ushered upstairs and into the temporary bathroom, where he came upon Bessie's naked body. Still in the bath, with her head partially submerged, she was facing upwards. There was very little the doctor could do, although he did make a valiant attempt at artificial respiration.

It was to Dr French that Smith gave the first and doubtless well-rehearsed account of what he claimed has taken place on that tragic morning. According to Smith, the couple had got out of bed at about 7.30a.m., with Smith going out more or less immediately to purchase some fresh fish. Upon his return, approximately half an hour later, he called out to his wife but received no reply. After a brief search of each room, he found her in the bath and in the same state as Dr French had found her. Asked why he had failed to pull her free of the bath, he declared her to be too heavy. A feeble excuse but, in the stress of the moment, it did not excite undue attention.

Perhaps, at this point, it should be asked why Dr French's suspicions failed to be aroused. Having seen Bessie on two occasions and clearly seeing no proof of a fit, he seems to have accepted this latest turn of events without demur. Indeed, at the subsequent inquest it was his evidence that helped ensure neither an autopsy nor the suggestion that Smith was anything less than the loving husband who had done everything necessary to save his wife.

Yet, before levelling too many criticisms at the doctor, it should also be mentioned that French had no idea that the man he knew as Henry Williams had anything to gain by his wife's death. To use his own words:

> Two people walk into my consulting room and tell me a tale that is consistent with epilepsy. At the time I have to put some leading questions, but I have no reason to suppose that there is any suspicion attaching to them. However, I get the information which leads me to suppose that it sounds like epilepsy that this woman is suffering from. It is not wonderful that I do not see her in a fit, because in nine cases out of ten when you are

> first consulted about an epileptic attack you do not see the patient in a fit. I am called in a day and a half afterwards, and again I do not see her in a fit, but her condition is not inconsistent with that of a person who has had a fit recently. The following day I am called in, and I find her drowned in a bath. Again, I have no suspicion; I have no reason for suspicion that there is foul play.

When the doctor realized that nothing further could be done, the local police constable was summoned. Having inspected the body and viewed the bath, he wrote down the following particulars, which more or less confirm what Smith had already told Dr French:

> His wife's name was Bessie Constance Annie, aged 35 years. They both got up together at 7.30a.m. that morning, and he went out to get some fish. He returned about eight o'clock, unlocking the door, went into the dining room and called his wife. Getting no reply he went into the bedroom that they used on the same floor, but she was not there. He then went upstairs to the back bedroom and found the deceased in the bath with her head under water. He raised her head and spoke to her, but got no reply. He then went for Dr French, who came almost immediately and assisted him to lift her out of the bath. The doctor applied artificial respiration, but to no avail.

The inquest, which was held on the following Monday, saw Smith playing the part of the distraught husband. On several occasions tears were seen on his face, a factor that helped him gain the sympathy of both coroner and jury. What else could explain their total acceptance of his story – a story which, if considered in detail, is full of contradictions?

First and foremost there is the question of the position of the bath and the time it took to fill it with water. It has already been noted that Smith had had to purchase a portable bath which he had placed in an upstairs bedroom. It was a highly inconvenient arrangement as the only water supply was in the kitchen. Anyone wishing to take a bath would be forced to carry a series of buckets up the full flight of stairs.

According to later calculations, simply getting the bath half full would require twelve journeys, and to get it three-quarters full would mean twenty journeys. It took a minute and a half to fill the bucket, and two minutes to carry it upstairs and empty it. A further thirty-five minutes would also be taken with the lighting and heating of the copper which was required to get the water to boiling-point.

All this, so Smith had declared, was undertaken not by himself but by Bessie during his thirty minutes absence! Given that Bessie was supposed to be unwell, supposedly suffering from occasional fits, it becomes doubly clear that the task was impossible. It is far more likely that Smith had prepared the bath sometime earlier, probably telling his wife that a bath would do her good. Who was she to argue?

A second point that the jury failed to consider was Smith's rather stupid declaration that his wife was too heavy for him to pull out of the bath. This just does not make sense. Bessie was not a particularly large woman, whilst Smith appears to have been relatively fit. Anyone coming across a similar situation would certainly have attempted to remove the body as quickly as possible so as to administer some form of artificial respiration. If all else failed, he could simply have emptied the bath. Intead, he left her unsupported, so allowing her to slip once more under the surface of the water. It does not seem to have crossed the mind of the coroner that Bessie could have died during the short interval in which Smith had gone to fetch the doctor.

Then there was the matter of the soap that Bessie was clutching at the time of her death. If she had been suffering from some kind of epileptic fit, she would have released this piece of soap as the muscles in her hand began to relax. Instead, she seems to have held on more tightly, a clear case of a drowning woman clutching at the nearest equivalent to a straw. According to Rutley Mowll, coroner for East Kent, the soap was seen as evidence that supported Smith's version of events. In his summing-up of the situation, Mowll asked whether Bessie was drowned by accident or by violence. He then went on to answer the question in such a way as to lead the jury to pass a verdict of death by misadventure: 'If she had been drowned by violence they would have expected to find some signs of a struggle, and they would not have expected to find a piece of soap in her right hand; to have the soap was a natural thing for anyone who was having a bath, but it would be a very unnatural circumstance with anyone who had been struggling in the water with someone else.'

Having escaped detection, Smith quickly took up the matter of Bessie's funeral. Alfred Hogbin, local undertaker, house-furnisher and ironmonger, whose premises were then situated on the corner of William Street and the High Street, was contacted by Smith on the day of the drowning. Hogbin had, in fact, already had dealings with Smith, being responsible for selling him a number of items of furniture that had been required for the newly rented house. (In following the footsteps of George Joseph Smith, it is fairly easy to locate the original site of Hogbin's premises, known as Victoria House, but the shop has since been demolished. Instead, the area holds a series of smaller retail units whose building was completed in 1989.)

The hastily arranged funeral was carried out on Tuesday, the earliest possible day. Smith's instructions were precise and to the point, showing no real feeling for the victim from whose will he would soon profit. He had simply told Hogbin that the funeral should be carried out as quickly as possible. As a result, Bessie was unceremoniously laid in the Herne Bay cemetery, her grave not even marked.

From Smith's point of view, the funeral was a mere inconvenience. Far more important was the proving of the will, a matter that he was to leave in the hands of Philip Annesley. It is interesting to note that Annesley himself later recalled that Smith was in a very unsettled state during the week that followed the murder. Was it a sign of guilt or fear? Either way, the usually mild-mannered solicitor had to order Smith to pull himself together, having never seen anyone in that condition of agitation.

Someone else who was confronted by Smith during the immediate aftermath of the funeral was Carrie Rapley. It was on the morning of the funeral that he re-entered her small office in the front room of Grosvenor House. He had come to pay a further instalment on the rent. Striding straight up to her raised desk, he immediately bent his head down and began to sob. Carrie later recalled that day's conversation to a packed Old Bailey courtroom.

'Has anything happened?' Carrie asked.

'Have you not heard? She is dead.'

'Who is dead?' came her second question.

'My wife.' Smith confided. 'She had a fit during the week. I went out. She went to have a bath, and she must have had another fit, for when I came back I found her dead in the bath.'

Although Carrie was surprised by these revelations, they could not possibly compare with Smith's next remark.

'Was it not a jolly good job I got her to make her will?'

Clearly Smith could not understand the total silence which this question received. Flustered and angry, he continued to pursue the point.

'Well, is it not the correct thing when people marry for the wife to make her will and leave everything to her husband, and her husband to make his will and leave everything to his wife?'

'Did you make yours?' Carrie finally enquired.

'Yes.'

'I thought you had told me you had not got anything?' she queried.

'Oh well, I made my will all the same,' came the reply, as Smith tried to wriggle out of the difficulty he had created for himself.

Not surprisingly, George Joseph Smith departed the town of Herne Bay towards the end of July. Before doing so he had already made contact with a certain Edith Pegler, telling her to meet him at Margate.

So far, of course, nothing has been said of this woman. Bearing in mind the way he normally treated women, Edith Pegler had a very peculiar relationship with Smith. Unlike any other woman in his life, he never once tried to cheat her out of money. After each of his exploits that variously involved jilting, marrying and killing other women, he always returned to her. She, for her part, never appears to have suspected him of leading a double life.

On each of the occasions on which Smith disappeared, often for months on end, he would simply tell her that he was travelling around the country buying and selling antiques. This story also helped him explain the sudden increase in affluence that always resulted from these various travels. As for the story he told her to explain that unusually long absence during the spring and early summer of 1912, he informed Edith that he had gone to Canada. As always she believed him, looking upon his heavily suntanned face as obvious proof of this fact. If she had thought about it, such a tan was far more likely to be achieved in south-east England, where daily summer temperatures had regularly peaked at 80°F.

Using the names Mr and Mrs Smith, it seems likely that Smith and Edith Pegler took rooms somewhere near Margate High Street. The exact address is unknown, Smith never choosing to use it in any official document. But it was still necessary for him to receive correspondence in the name of Henry Williams. For this purpose he approached a newsagent at 158 High Street, arranging with the owner to receive letters addressed to that name. Clearly he was intending to keep enquiries from Herne Bay at arm's length, whilst denying Edith the opportunity of learning anything of the activities in which he had been involved.

The couple remained at Margate for only a few days, moving on to Tunbridge Wells. No definite reason for this hurried move can be established, although Smith himself informed Annesley that it was for the purpose of buying antiques. Having arrived at Tunbridge Wells, he made an arrangement similar to that previously established at Margate. Accommodation was found, this time in a boarding house on the corner of Grosvenor and Hanover Roads, whilst a newsagent (at 25 Grove Hill Road) was also approached for the taking-in of letters, with one penny being paid for each letter received and collected.

Remaining at Tunbridge Wells for a somewhat lengthier period of time, the couple eventually quit the county of Kent in September. For Smith, it was not to prove a final break with the county, 'the Brides in the Bath Murderer' being forced to return in August 1915. During the intervening three years he continued his career of lying and cheating, entering into a further three marriages. Relatively lucky was a certain Alice Reavil, who merely lost her life savings. Two other women, Alice Burnham and Margaret Lofty, were considerably less fortunate. On marrying them, he arranged to take out life-insurance policies in their name. Murdering both of them, he was then able to claim fairly large sums of money from the respective companies he had used.

Lacking both imagination and common sense, Smith used the same method to kill as that he had previously employed at Herne Bay. Because of this, suspicion was eventually aroused. In January 1915 Charles Burnham, whose daughter Alice had been murdered at Blackpool thirteen months earlier, came across this item in the *News of the World*:

Bride's Tragic Fate on Day after Wedding

> Particularly sad circumstances under which a bride of a day met her death were investigated at an Islington inquest on Margaret Elizabeth Lloyd, thirty-eight, wife of a land agent of Holloway. The husband said he was married to deceased at Bath. After travelling to London she complained of a headache and giddiness, and he took her to a medical man who prescribed for her. The following morning she said she felt much better, and during the day she went out shopping. At 7.30 she said she would have a bath, and she then appeared cheerful. A quarter of an hour later witness went out, and returned at a quarter past eight, expecting to see her in the sitting room. As she was not there he inquired of the landlady, and they went to the bathroom which was in darkness. He lit the gas and then found his wife under the water, the bath being three parts full. The next day witness found a letter amongst deceased's clothing, but there was nothing in it to suggest that she was likely to take her life.

Noticing a number of points that seemed identical to the drowning of his own daughter in a bath, Charles Burnham brought the matter to the attention of the local police at Aylesbury. An immediate investigation soon revealed that the Henry Williams who had married the deceased Bessie Mundy, the George Smith who had married the deceased Alice Burnham and the John Lloyd who had married the deceased Elizabeth Lofty were, in fact, one and the same person.

The subsequent trial, which took place at the Old Bailey in June 1915, saw George Joseph Smith tried for the wilful murder of Bessie Mundy. With little more than circumstantial evidence being mustered against him, there were continual references to both the other women he had married who had mysteriously died in their baths. Although this was a rather unsatisfactory way of bringing a prosecution, it was necessary in this case in order to provide evidence of a system. The jury, after hearing the evidence from Herne Bay, Blackpool and Islington retired for only twenty-two minutes before finding Smith guilty.

Smith's return to the county of Kent in August 1915 was a direct result of that verdict. Having found him guilty of wilful murder, Mr Justice Scrutton, the High Court judge directed to hear the trial, ordered that he should be taken to 'His Majesty's prison at Maidstone' where he should be 'hanged by the neck' until he was dead. It was a sentence that seems to have taken Smith completely by surprise. Despite the weight of evidence against him, he remained throughout the trial convinced that the jury would find him not guilty. Even more surprising, he also seems to have convinced himself that he was innocent. As the foreman of the jury pronounced their findings, his face went deathly pale.

Yet, despite all that had happened, Smith continued to believe in and plead his own innocence. Not once did he admit his guilt, claiming the death of each wife to be a straightforward accident and not of his making. On the day of his execution he had literally to be dragged to the scaffold. With his arms pinioned down by his side, he screamed out, 'I am innocent! I am innocent!'

Prior to that final appointment with the hangman, he even went some way in convincing a leading Church dignitary of his innocence. This was Dr Pereira, the Bishop of Croydon, who visited Smith whilst he was at Maidstone. The Bishop later provided this account of the meeting: 'He told me – not under seal of confession – that for twenty years he had been a most wicked and abandoned man; that he had been steeped in every villainy, but never of murder. He knew that there was no chance of a reprieve, nor did he desire it. He deserved his fate. But again, he asserted, with tears coursing down his cheeks, that he had not had anything to do with the murder of these three women. He left a statement to this effect in his cell ... I cannot with a long experience of penitents, believe that he was not sincere in his declarations ...' Make of this what you will!

In fact, it may well suggest that George Joseph Smith was now suffering from schizophrenia: the innocent Smith doing his best to distance himself from the evil-doing of the guilty Smith. If this was the case, he probably believed in his own innocence and, as a result, appeared sincere in his proclamations of innocence. Further evidence for this supposition comes from a letter he wrote just four days before his execution. Addressed to Edith Pegler, it adopted a style totally different from those terse little missives he had used on a number of earlier occasions:

> Dear Love, Your pure heart and conscience free from stain helps me to believe that, whilst memory holds a seat within your sacred brow you will remember me. You are the last person in the world to whom I shall write, in as much as this is my last letter. I could write volumes of pathos prompted by the cruel position wherein I am now placed. But I have too much respect and love for your feelings to do so. I have not asked for a reprieve, nor made a petition, and do not intend doing so. Since we have failed to obtain justice from the earthly judges, I prefer death rather than imprisonment. So an innocent man goes to his untimely end, a victim of cruel fate. God alone is my Judge and the King of kings. It was He who gave me life, who

> ordained our coming together. My property I give to you. Don't be alone on the last day, when I shall have left this weary ark behind, where perjury, malice, spite, vindictiveness, prejudice and all other earthly ills will have done its best, and can harm me no more. My time is occupied in solemn and deep meditation. I am preparing my Soul for him to receive. I return to the teaching I received from my mother ... I shall have an extraordinary peace, perfect peace. May an old age, serene and bright, and as lovely as a Lapland night, lead thee to thy grave. Now my true love, goodbye until we meet again.
> Yours, with immortal love,
> George.

George Joseph Smith was executed early on the morning of Friday 13 August 1915.

Maidstone prison must represent the final destination for anyone who has chosen to pursue Smith's footsteps beyond the bounds of Herne Bay. Within those grim outer walls, little changed since 1915, his interred body is still retained. In common with that of Bessie Mundy, it lies in an unmarked grave, and only the prison register indicates the final resting-place of 'the Brides in the Bath Murderer.'

– 6 –
A Deadly Crossing-Point,
Challock Hill,
1932

Thirty-five years of age and happily married to Thomas Stemp, the licensee of the White Hart Hotel, Wadhurst, Sussex, Janie Stemp, was, in one respect, a very unusual woman: she had a passion for driving. It was something which, in 1932, set her apart from most of her female contemporaries. Few women, at that time, were to be seen behind the wheel of a car, the vast majority dependent on public transport. Janie, however, was not only in possession of a car but much preferred the freedom of the open road. It was a pleasure that beggared description. For this reason she was frequently to be seen driving along the narrow lanes of the Kent and Sussex border.

With the onset of summer, Janie persuaded her husband that it was a good time to purchase a new car. For many years it had been her ambition to drive a sports car, and recently she had seen the automobile of her dreams. It was a Hornet Special. Built by the firm of Wolsey, its design included a low-slung chassis which supported a six-cylinder 47hp engine capable of taking the car to a speed of seventy miles an hour!

In terms of looks, this was a very fetching piece of machinery and clearly superior to most other vehicles found on those congestion-free roads of the early thirties. Instead of the all-black finish that was the hallmark of most mass-produced cars, this particular vehicle had a gleaming silver body and endearing dark blue wings. Its charms were truly irresistible.

Apart from good looks and a useful turn of speed, the Wolsey Hornet was also blessed with a low price tag. Selling at under £200, it was well within the family budget. In fact, most of the money the Stemps required was raised from the sale of a larger family saloon which Thomas had bought a few years earlier.

In persuading her husband to buy a sports car, Janie could not be accused of ignoring the needs of her family. Unlike many similar cars, this one was a four-seater. As a result, it could comfortably carry Thomas and Janie and their two school-aged children.

As soon as Janie had taken possession of the car, she started to plan a series of summer trips that would include family picnics and several visits to the seaside. Most ambitious of all was a run down to Aldershot, where the two children, thirteen-year-old Peggy and eight-year-old Geoffrey, could enjoy the sights and sounds of the annual military tattoo.

Someone else enjoying a new-found freedom during that early part of 1932 was twenty-six-year-old James Thomas Collins. In December of the previous year he had been released from prison, having served a fifteen-month sentence for a rather serious crime. It appears that during the autumn of 1931 he had entered a London shooting gallery and, for reasons best known to himself, had proceeded to fire one of the guns into the surrounding crowd. Two people had been seriously injured as a result of this mad spree.

It may well have been Collins' fascination with guns that had led to this awful crime. As much as Janie loved cars, Collins appeared to love rifles. Without them, his new-found freedom would seem quite meaningless. For this reason he decided to join the Army, being recruited into the 2nd Battalion of the East Kent Regiment. Not surprisingly, he failed to mention his recent conviction, telling the recruiting officer that he was a merchant seaman recently returned from Canada.

Not that Collins was a stranger to the Army. He had previously joined the ranks in 1926 but had subsequently deserted. Possibly he could have remained free, had he not carried out a series of burglaries that resulted in his arrest by the police. Upon confessing that he was a deserter, he was handed over to the military authorities and spent a short spell in the 'glasshouse'.

A further brush with the law followed in April 1927. Having been discharged from the Army, Collins turned to car theft. Again, he proved singularly unsuccessful, his first and only attempt resulting in a six-month prison sentence.

On coming out of gaol, it is possible that he planned on turning over a new leaf. Joining the merchant navy, he proceeded to work his passage to New York. However, the attractions of that city proved too much, and he jumped ship. Unable to stay out of trouble for long, he soon found himself under arrest. This time the charge was illegal possession of firearms. After another short spell behind bars, he was returned to Britain, where he again fell foul of the law, this time as a result of the London shooting-gallery incident.

Having joined the East Kents, a regiment always known as 'the Buffs', Private Collins was dispatched to the regimental barracks at Shorncliffe. At first all went remarkably well. He managed to keep himself out of trouble and was soon in a position to demonstrate his remarkable shooting skills. In March, for instance, he was awarded a special medal that carried the words: 'Argyll Squad, 19-3-32, Buffs Highest Score Rifle, Pte Collins'.

At Wadhurst, some forty miles from Shorncliffe, Janie Stemp continued to take advantage of her newly purchased Wolsey Hornet Special. Every day she would take the car out for a short spin, the deep-throated engine producing a more or less trouble-free performance. If there was a problem, it concerned a slight oil loss. But that could be fixed in the near future.

As Peggy's half-term school holiday approached, the two children were promised a special treat. They were told that Janie's mother, Mrs Swift, would be staying for the weekend. They loved their grandmother and looked forward to a perfect few days.

Mrs Swift, who was also called Janie, was sixty-nine years old and as fashion-conscious as her daughter. One photograph, taken in the 1920s, shows her wearing a short, flowing coat and a then-fashionable cloche hat. Her husband, like her daughter's, was in the pub and hotel trade. He was the licensee of Ye Olde Sportsman at Seasalter.

In this same month of June, No. 6285020 Private James Thomas Collins of the 2nd Battalion The Buffs, was given a further opportunity to demonstrate his shooting skills. At that time, some of the newer recruits had been detailed to the nearby rifle range at Hythe, where they were given further instructions in the use of the standard .303 rifle.

Despite his love of guns, which had prompted him to join, or rather re-join, the British Army, Collins was beginning to feel a little restless. He, too, enjoyed the freedom of the open road. The result was that at sometime around 4a.m. on the morning of Monday 3 June, a good hour or more before 'reveille', he decided to leave Hythe camp. Slipping on his Army uniform but deciding to dispense with belt and puttees, he exchanged his heavy leather boots for a pair of lightweight canvas shoes. Making his way to the tent flap, he decided to take one further item – a service rifle.

Even at that early hour of the morning, this particular June day showed every sign of being a glorious example of what a summer's day should be like. Glancing out across the English Channel (the rifle range borders a long sandy beach to the south-west of Hythe), Collins could see a number of distant vessels and one or two fishing-boats. Doubtless it reminded him of his earliest association with the merchant navy and his run-in with the New York police. Walking along the beach towards Hythe and then on to Sandgate, he eventually scrambled over the cliffs and joined the main road which leads to Ashford.

Private Collins had once again deserted the British Army.

At Wadhurst, sometime around midday, Janie Stemp, preparing to drive her mother back to Seasalter, placed a few last-minute items in the family's Hornet Special. Since it was such a pleasant day, it was decided that the journey should be made with the hood down. On that Monday Geoffrey had returned to his school in Tonbridge, but Peggy was still on holiday, so she joined the two women, electing to make herself comfortable on one of the rear seats. To make the journey more pleasant than it might normally be, the three of them decided to stop somewhere around Challock for a picnic.

As for Private Collins, undertaking his own personal route march, midday saw him on the outskirts of Ashford. In all, he had been on the road for about eight hours, making only an occasional stop at the side of the busy A20. Most of the traffic was heading towards Folkestone, numerous day-trippers having decided to spend a few pleasant hours on the town promenade or strolling along the short pier. As they passed him by, a number idly stared at Collins. Some probably pitied him, feeling it to be unjust that the Army should demand that he undertake such an exhausting journey on this warm, sunny afternoon. Others, somewhat more knowledgeable, may have wondered why he lacked a backpack and was not in full uniform.

Skirting around the east side of Ashford, Collins entered the village of Kennington, where he came across Grace Swift and her niece, Nancy Garland. Both were standing on the pathway and looking at a dead mole.

'I wondered what you were looking at madam,' indicated Collins as he also stopped and looked at the object.

'What are you doing, young man?' Grace enquired. 'Are you going shooting?'

Unfortunately, Grace was much nearer the truth than she realized. But at this point, Collins still appeared relatively good-humoured.

'Yes,' he replied. 'Just a few rabbits!'

In fact, Grace Swift and her niece were at that point talking to a man who was about to commit a random murder with little or no motive. These two women were fortunate that it was not they who were to be his victims. Indeed, Collins seems to have taken a certain liking to them.

'Do you mind if I walk with you?' he asked.

'Not at all,' replied Grace.

The three of them continued in the direction of Eastwell Towers, Collins' intentions being to join the A251. Upon reaching this road, they parted company, the armed deserter now striking out for Challock.

By now the silver-and-blue sports car and its three occupants were also on the outskirts of Ashford. Passing quickly through this busy town, they too joined the A251. Then, as now, this is a fairly narrow road that offers a number of fine views across the Wye Downs. But it was not this that attracted the attention of the driver and her two passengers. As the car sped towards Challock at a comfortable forty miles an hour, their attention was drawn to the figure of a soldier determinedly marching in the same direction, a rifle slung over his left shoulder. As they drew level with him, Janie gradually took her foot off the accelerator and de-clutched into a lower gear.

'You're making a good walk of it,' she called out. The others in the car laughed.

The thoughts running through the mind of Private Collins can only be guessed. Possibly he was embarrassed by this uninvited attention. Perhaps he put a hand to his rifle, or maybe he interpreted their good humour for mockery, and somehow wished to take his revenge. Alternatively, as he had now been walking for about eight hours, he might well have felt envious of such a luxurious-looking car. Either way, he just scowled whilst the sports car accelerated into the distance.

Collins, for his part, continued his own lengthy journey, his mind now made up. Somehow he would get to London.

Janie Stemp continued driving for a further half mile. As they approached the summit of Challock Hill, they slowed down once again. To the right lay Eastwell Park with its continuous four-mile wall, whilst to the left was King's Wood. It was an ideal place for the proposed picnic. Seeing a suitable lay-by, they drove onto the other side of the road and parked on the verge of the woods. Sharing round the meat sandwiches and soft drinks, they began to relax.

Behind them, somewhere on that long road, a dishevelled and tired soldier continued his extraordinary twenty-mile walk. Already he had passed through Seabrook, Sellindge, Smeeth, Willesborough, Boughton Lees and Eastwell. At 1.30 in the afternoon, having reached King's Wood, he came upon the silver-and-blue sports car that had given him so much attention some fifteen minutes earlier. His thoughts are difficult to comprehend. Possibly he was thinking of revenge – or maybe he just wanted the car.

Overcome by some crazy notion, he snatched the rifle from his shoulder, removed the safety catch and inserted a bullet. There was a resounding crash as he pulled the trigger. Janie Stemp, who was standing close to the car, suddenly fell to the ground. A bullet had caught her in the chest, passing straight through and out the other side. She was dead within seconds. Further bullets were unleashed upon Janie Swift and Peggy, both of whom were still seated in the car. They, too, died instantly.

Although the A251 was not a particularly busy road, Collins could still consider himself fortunate that no cars happened to be passing at that point in time. However, he was not going to leave anything else to chance. Leaving both Peggy and Janie Swift in the position in which they had died, he pulled Janie Stemp some thirty feet into the undergrowth, depositing the corpse on its back. As he did so, he heard the heavy rumble of a lorry and a passing bus. Would the driver of either of the vehicles stop to investigate? If they did, they would have no doubts as to exactly what had taken place.

As it happens, neither vehicle stopped. The driver of the lorry, Horace Franks of Ospringe, certainly noticed the stationary sports car. Seeing Peggy in the back seat, with her head over the side, and Janie Swift slopped forward in the front passenger seat, he merely assumed that they were asleep. Certainly he saw no reason as to why he should stop.

The fright Collins received from hearing the lorry prompted him to move the car. In his panic he seems to have fumbled over the starting key and the unusually short gear-stick that was fitted to this type of vehicle. Indeed, later evidence was to reveal that Collins made at least three attempts to start the engine. Eventually he managed to get the car moving, taking it a further 800 yards along the road to a second lay-by where he could actually get it under the cover of some trees. The site he had chosen was about half a mile from Challock crossroads and was the starting-point of what was then a footpath to White Hill. Quickly scrambling out of the car, he opened the single passenger door and dragged the lifeless body of the older Janie into the woods. Here, he deposited her body on an embankment to the right of the White Hill footpath. The lighter body of Peggy was carried rather than dragged and placed a few feet along a second path that ran to the right.

Returning to the car, he re-started the engine, clumsily reversing it back onto the Challock Road. As he pulled away from the leafy glade, the sports car deposited some oil. Janie had still not taken it into the garage to have the seal repaired.

Continuing in a northward direction, Collins passed over the crossroads at Challock, heading towards Faversham and then on to London. That he was still in something of a panic can be surmised by various reports on his driving. In Challock village an AA patrolman, Frank Post, considered he was driving far too fast, whilst John Hughes, an insurance agent, noted that the car was on the wrong side of the road as it passed through Ospringe.

However, no further indication of Collins' progress was made until he reached Camberwell in London. Being unfamiliar with the car he was driving, he was unaware of the oil problem. The engine suddenly seized. For the last twenty miles, in fact, there had been insufficient oil in the engine for it to register on the gauge.

Wishing in some way to conceal the car and finding himself close to a garage on Denmark Hill, Collins summoned the owner, Eric Spencer, asking him to provide some assistance. Both of them walked over to the vehicle.

'Is it yours then?', asked the garage proprietor.

'No,' replied Collins, who seemed ready for the question. 'It belongs to my officer.'

Spencer examined the car and noted a large hole in the side of the crank case and a connecting-rod torn from the crank shaft. He judged the engine to be practically ruined, the damage consistent with the car's having been driven without oil.

'We'll have to push the car to the garage,' Spencer suggested.

With that small task complete, the garage owner took out his notebook, to write down a few details.

'Now, who are you?' he asked.

'Jackson,' came Collins' carefully considered reply. 'Private J.T. Jackson of the 2nd Battalion Buffs.'

'And who owns the car?'

'Lieutenant D.L. Wates, also of the Buffs,' Collins lied. 'You can get hold of him at Shorncliffe Barracks. I was supposed to meet him with the car at Victoria station.'

With these details noted, Collins indicated that he would have to remove a few things from the car. These included a rifle, travelling-rug and small suitcase. As these items were taken out, it became obvious that the dark stains that Spencer had previously seen were bloodstains.

'What caused them?' he asked with surprise.

'Oh, nothing to worry about,' replied Collins, who appeared to be quite unconcerned by the question. 'I was joy-riding with a girl. She cut herself on a glass.' To prove the point, he nodded towards a broken tumbler. 'Don't tell my officer. He knows nothing about the girl. I'd be in serious trouble if he found out.'

'So where is she now?' persisted Spencer.

'We stopped off at a doctor's. He insisted on detaining her. She'll be all right after a rest.'

Despite having seen evidence of the murder, the garage-owner's suspicions were not aroused. It was quite frequent for cars, involved in a crash or other type of accident, to enter his garage, many of them having similar stains on the upholstery. Besides, Collins' explanation was not totally implausible.

Meanwhile, at Challock, the first of the three bodies had been discovered. At 2.45 a Maidstone and District bus, on a regular route between Faversham and Ashford, passed along the King's Wood stretch of the A251. Looking along the line of trees, the driver caught a fleeting glimpse of a young woman lying face down. He was uncertain as to whether she was in difficulty but chose to mention it to the relief driver upon reaching Ashford. The relief driver and his conductor, following exactly the same route, saw nothing on the outward journey, arriving at Faversham an hour later. However, at 4.45, as the bus again passed King's Wood, both driver and conductor saw the young woman in exactly the same position as had been described to them. Fearing something was terribly wrong, they got out to investigate. Approaching the body, they realized from the heavily bloodstained clothes that there was little chance of her still being alive. Not wishing to disturb the ground any further, they abandoned the scene and drove the bus non-stop to Boughton Lees, where their grisly discovery was reported to the police.

In fact, the relief crew had discovered the body of Peggy Stemp. Apparently she had been deposited in such a way that she could be seen only from the higher viewing position afforded by a large passenger bus. This certainly explains why none of the drivers of at least fifty or sixty cars was to report seeing anything unusual.

The arrival of the Kent County Constabulary resulted in a wider search of the area that led to the discovery of a second body, that of Peggy's grandmother. It was not to be for several hours that a third body was to be found, the police having no reason to search further afield. That they did so resulted from information given to them by Challock villager Honor Campbell.

Earlier in the day she had been a passenger on the 1.45 bus. This was the one that Collins had heard whilst disposing of Janie Stemp's body. As it passed the sports car parked in the lay-by, she noticed the two female passengers. Unlike the lorry-driver, Horace Franks, she did not think they were asleep. To her, they had a 'deathly pale' appearance, as if both of them were very ill. Mentioning this to the police, who were then questioning all villagers, she described how one of the two women was slumped over the side and the other had fallen forward onto the front passenger seat. At the time she assumed they had been involved in a road accident and that the driver had gone to inform the police.

For the detectives called to the scene of these murders, Honor Campbell's account was to prove extremely useful. Not only could she describe the car but, from her description of where it had been parked, it appeared to be in a lay-by different from the one closest to where the two bodies had been found.

Seeing the possibility of this second site's providing additional clues that might help in discovering the identity of either the victims or the murderer, a number of constables were ordered to widen out the original search. Within a short while they were to report the discovery of a third body, that of Janie Stemp.

Aware that they were dealing with a killer who might well strike again, the Kent police instituted a massive county-wide search. Although they had unearthed precious little that would help them, they did have one possible report that might be worth checking out. This concerned a deserter from the Buffs. According to information given to the police, this man had absconded from the rifle range at Hythe. Of somewhat greater significance, however, was that the report also indicated that this deserter had taken with him an Army-issue rifle. Whilst there was nothing to connect him with the triple murder at Challock, the man would certainly have to be found. If nothing else, he had to be eliminated from police inquiries.

Collins, by this time, was beginning to make a few inept efforts at covering his tracks. Having convinced the garage proprietor that the bloodstains represented nothing very serious, he had then headed for Finsbury Park station, where he deposited the suitcase he had taken out of the car. Belonging, as it did, to Janie Swift, it contained those various items she had required for her recent ill-fated weekend at Wadhurst.

From Finsbury Park, Collins took a bus to Broad Street, where he made a telephone call to Scotland Yard. Making contact with one of the duty officers, he blurted down the phone the chilling words, 'There is a dead woman with a motor car between Ashford and Chatham, by the roadside.' Then, as an after-thought, 'You better not ignore me.' Refusing to give his name, Collins slammed down the receiver. The reasons for this telephone call are totally incomprehensible. Presumably Collins did have some sort of reason.

From Broad Street, Collins walked on to Haringay. It seems that he had now decided to make for the Barnet area, his parents having a house somewhere close to this town. Possibly he had thoughts of hiding out in the family home, waiting long enough for the police search to die down. Certainly his wanderings now appear to be a lot more purposeful, some of that original walk lacking the directness of someone whose intentions had always been to reach London. Indeed, it is quite possible that, on first setting out, Collins had no clear idea as to where he was headed. Having reached Haringay, however, he then caught a bus to New Southgate and walked to Osidge Lane. Here, close to exhaustion, he slipped over the wall of a sewage farm, choosing to rest for a few hours.

At one o'clock on the morning of 14 June Police Constable Sidney Chapman of Barnet's 'Y' Division was wheeling his bike along Cockfosters Road. One of a handful of policemen who regularly patrolled this area by night, he was a little concerned about the man he saw in the distance. For one thing, it was rare to see people on the streets this late. More worrying however, was the object the stranger carried over his shoulder. Although it was wrapped, it had the distinctive shape of a rifle.

Collins, the man in question, had also seen PC Chapman. As they approached one another, Collins decided to avoid the confrontation that appeared more than certain. Noticing a convenient side street leading off to the left, he slipped down this road and began to walk a little faster. It was a stupid thing to do. Whilst he might once have stood a chance of persuading Chapman as to his honesty, this now was a most unlikely possibility.

Having seen this manœuvre and realizing it was designed to avoid meeting the patrolling constable, Chapman mounted his bike and rode after the fugitive. He soon drew level.

'What have you on your shoulder?' Chapman challenged in a firm and uncompromising voice.

'Do you want to see it?' asked Collins.

'Yes, please,' was the constable's response.

'Are you sure you want to see it?' Collins prevaricated.

'Certainly.'

Collins then proceeded to remove the cover, but instead of allowing the constable to see the gun, he suddenly thrust the barrel straight at the officer's chest. Murder number four was now on the cards.

'Stand there or I'll shoot you dead!'

'Don't be foolish!' warned Chapman. 'Don't point that gun at me! What's the matter?'

'I have shot a man on the plain.' (Collins was lying but possibly referring to the plain at Shorncliffe.)

At first Chapman was not particularly concerned about the situation. It was not that unusual for a police officer to be threatened. However, there was something very unusual about Collins. According to Chapman, it was his eyes. They constantly stared – it was almost as if Collins was inhuman. Perhaps, after all, this particular villain was capable of pulling the trigger. Chapman did not feel at all safe. In an attempt to defuse the situation, he tried to befriend Collins. Instead of cajoling and warning, he resorted to ordinary topics of conversation.

'Where are you going?' asked Chapman as an opening gambit.

'Barnet!' snapped Collins.

'No, surely not,' continued the officer. 'You're going the wrong way.'

'Not for East Barnet, where I live,' replied Collins. 'It's most unfortunate you've met me.'

'Why?' continued the constable. 'Surely you're not going to shoot me?'

'Why not?'

'I haven't done you any harm.'

'If you hadn't stopped me, I'd be in Barnet by now,' declared Collins rather optimistically. 'I shall have the hangman's rope around my neck in three days' time!'

'Are you a Territorial?' asked Chapman, trying to change the topic.

'No,' Collins replied. 'I belong to the 2nd Battalion of the Buffs. We're stationed at Shorncliffe.'

In all, the conversation went on for about twenty minutes. Feeling a little more confident, PC Chapman attempted to move nearer the gun, hoping to snatch it away. It was a move that was quickly countered, Collins warning the policeman to keep his hands firmly on the bike. It was shortly after this that Collins decided to continue his journey towards Barnet. To Chapman he now issued a further warning, telling him that if he followed he would certainly be shot. Bravely, the constable chose to ignore the threat, keeping his eye on Collins from a discreet distance.

After a few minutes, the tired and exasperated Collins

turned to face the policeman. Putting the rifle to his shoulder and covering the trigger, he issued one final warning.

'If you follow me, I'll shoot you!'

'Drop your gun,' ordered Chapman. 'Don't be a fool! Don't shoot!'

Not wishing to take matters further, Collins backed into some nearby trees and disappeared. Chapman, knowing himself to be safe, summoned help by sounding his regulation whistle.

Despite a massive search, nothing was seen of Collins until 7.30 the following morning. It was then that a police motor cyclist came across him on the outskirts of Barnet and quickly summoned assistance from others involved in the search. When Collins was chased into a nearby field, once more he began to load his rifle. As he did so, PC Ambrose Reedman worked his way behind him and crawled to within hailing distance.

'Stop!' he called out. 'Don't be a fool! Drop your rifle!'

Collins swung round, his gun ready and loaded. For one terrible moment Reedman thought that he was about to become the rifleman's next victim.

'Stand still, big boy!' Collins warned.

Reedman did exactly as he was told. For a few seconds Collins kept the rifle trained on Reedman. As he did so, he became increasingly aware that a number of other officers were moving towards him. Forgetting Reedman, he turned towards the main group and fired. His aim was deliberately high. Collins was simply warning them to keep back.

Those few moments were all that Reedman needed. Rushing forward, he sprang at Collins, knocking the rifle to the ground. Collins knew when he was beaten. Offering no further resistance, he told Reedman, 'That's about the lot.' Possibly he was referring to his supply of ammunition. Alternatively, he may have been referring to his own exhausted condition.

Placed under arrest, Collins was taken to Barnet police station, where he signed a full statement in which he admitted that he had 'no doubt' killed the three women whose car he had stolen. That he chose to use the words 'no doubt' was due to a complete loss of memory during the period of the actual shooting. In making his statement, Collins still made a sufficient admission to warrant his arrest for that crime: 'I had my rifle with me and twelve rounds of ammunition. I do not remember what happened afterwards, but they were killed and no doubt I did it. The next thing I remember was driving the car the women were in. I was covered with blood....'

Subsequently removed to Ashford, he was initially remanded by magistrates at the local police court. A few months later, James Thomas Collins was brought before the judge and jury at the autumn session of the Maidstone assize, where he put forward a plea of guilty but insane. To substantiate this defence, his counsel produced a considerable amount of evidence to demonstrate that he was not a sane and rational person. In particular the London shooting gallery incident was highlighted, as was an attempt to kill an ailing aunt when he turned on all the gas taps in her house. It was also mentioned that he had ridden on the buffers of a train, eventually throwing himself underneath the engine. Most convincing, perhaps, was the testimony of a senior prison officer, who indicated that at no time during his recent period of remand had Collins shown the slightest remorse for the crime he had committed.

The jury agreed with the defence plea and took only fifteen minutes to arrive at a verdict of 'insane'. To this they added a special commendation. They congratulated PC Reedman on his outstanding bravery in arresting Collins. The judge, in agreeing with the jury's commendation, also accepted their findings and sentenced Collins to be detained at 'His Majesty's pleasure'.

– 7 –
Once Seen, Never Forgotten,
Matfield,
1940

Before their final separation in March 1940, Dorothy and Walter Fisher would appear to have had a somewhat bizarre life-style. Having ceased sleeping with one another but remaining the closest of friends, each had taken a lover. In a very open form of relationship, each accepted that their spouse was being unfaithful, and even befriended each other's extra-marital partner.

It was Dorothy Fisher who seems to have taken the initiative. In 1934 she formed a sexual liaison with a Danish businessman named Westergaart. Already, by that date, the physical side of her relationship with Walter had become more or less non-existent, a state of affairs that seems to have resulted from the birth of their second daughter, Freda, some fifteen years earlier. Almost at once Walter accepted the inevitability of his wife's adultery, agreeing to Westergaart's frequent visits to their suburban home at Twickenham. Indeed, it is not beyond the realms of possibility that a temporary *ménage à trois* was established, with Dorothy and Westergaart spending an occasional night in each other's company while Walter retired to his own room and his own private thoughts.

As further proof of his acceptance of this relationship,

Walter, a successful London businessman, even went so far as to purchase Crittenden Cottage, a small rural retreat where his wife and her lover could spend time together in greater privacy. For such purposes, the cottage was ideal. Situated just outside the village of Matfield and surrounded by apple orchards and hop fields, there was little possibility of their being disturbed either by uninvited guests or by local village gossip.

As for the two daughters of the marriage, both of whom were now teenagers, it is difficult to assess the effect this relationship might have had upon them. Certainly they must have known what was going on – especially as they frequently joined their mother at the Matfield love-nest so charitably provided by their father.

In the meantime Walter Fisher must have been an extremely lonely man. Having now entered his mid-forties, he was caught in a sterile marriage that was dominated by his wife's desire to be with another man. For this reason it is not difficult to sympathize with his own entrance into an extra-marital attachment, and one that was soon mirroring Dorothy's relationship with Westergaart.

The new arrival into the Fisher *ménage* was the recently widowed Florence Iris Ransome. Considerably younger than Walter, being in her late twenties when they first met, she was the type of person who would always be noticed in a crowd, having short, soft auburn hair that gave her a distinctively attractive appearance. She was always expensively dressed. In particular, she favoured tailored suits, although for relaxing around the house she was more likely to choose a combination of fashionable beach-style trousers and tightly fitting multi-coloured jumpers. On all occasions, whether she was shopping, visiting friends or just lounging, her fingernails were always guaranteed to be perfectly manicured and covered in layers of thick red varnish.

The relationship between Walter Fisher and Iris Ransome, who for some reason he always referred to as 'Julie', quickly developed. Like Westergaart, she became a regular visitor at the Fishers' Twickenham house, whilst at weekends she and Walter would visit the Matfield cottage and spend a quiet weekend in each other's company.

This strange relationship entered a period of disruption when Florence became pregnant. Walter's feelings about this turn of events is unknown, but it seems that the new situation made him think about the possibility of setting up a separate home for the two of them. Despite Florence's suffering a miscarriage, he continued to pursue this idea, buying Carramore Farm, close to the Oxfordshire village of Piddington near Bicester. At first, Florence lived here on her own, using previously acquired secretarial skills to run the farm on Walter's behalf. As with his wife's continuing visits to Matfield, Walter would also slip down to Piddington, where he would spend an increasing number of weekends with Florence. During the week, however, both husband and wife would return to the family home.

In early 1940 the marriage finally collapsed. By this time Joan, the elder daughter, had married, and for this reason it seemed no longer necessary to maintain a large house in Twickenham. Dorothy went to live permanently at Crittenden Cottage, taking with her the now twenty-year-old Freda, together with Charlotte Saunders, a housemaid who seems to have survived the various comings and goings of Dorothy, Walter and their two paramours. Walter, for his part, having sold the house, moved permanently to Carramore Farm. Florence continued to run the farm while he commuted to London each day, travelling on the early morning train and not returning until late afternoon.

Despite the sale of the family home, husband and wife did not lose contact with one another, and the question of divorce was never considered. Indeed, the friendly relationship that had existed at Twickenham, was to continue, with Walter sometimes travelling to Matfield to spend a few hours with his estranged wife. Occasionally Florence would accompany him, Dorothy and Freda both welcoming her as an old friend. Indeed, there can be little doubt that Florence Ransome got on extremely well with Dorothy Fisher.

The frequency of those visits was eventually interrupted by a deteriorating international situation. The Fishers' original decision to separate had coincided with the final months of the 'phoney war'. During the next three months, Britain became increasingly embroiled in a conflict that saw German occupation of Norway, Denmark, Belgium and France in rapid succession.

Kent had been thrown into the front line of the war, and its inhabitants had to live with the very real possibility of invasion. Following upon the return of the British Expeditionary Force from Dunkirk, the fears of the county's populace were further excited by the necessity of evacuating thousands of school children. For the most part they were taken to Wales and the West Country, areas designated as beyond the range of the German bombers that would soon be operating from captured French airfields.

To bolster the country's defences, increasing numbers of troops and fighter aircraft were directed into the future battle zone. Most of the newly arrived soldiers were assigned either to the coastal area or to a line of rapidly constructed 'pillboxes' sited along the western bank of the River Medway. This, so 'the powers that be' had decided, was where a last-ditch stand would be made should the marauding German Panzers make that feared landing. As for the Royal Air Force, desperately short of Spitfires and Hurricanes, a few extra fighters were soon directed to Hawkinge, Manston, Biggin Hill and Eastchurch. As history clearly records, it was the valiant efforts of those who piloted these aircraft, together with the maintenance crews, that finally ensured that the troops on the ground were not to be called upon to face a relentless attack by the battle-hardened troops of Hitler's Wehrmacht.

Dorothy Fisher, living in the midst of this upheaval, was relatively unaffected. Although food was rationed and severe bombing predicted, those at Crittenden Cottage had little to fear. With over three acres of attached farmland, they would certainly not run out of food, whilst the possibility of an enemy aeroplane's choosing them as a target was about as remote as the Home Guard's getting uniforms by Christmas!

Only with regard to her relationship with Westergaart was Dorothy apparently affected by the war. As a Danish national, his movements were restricted. At one time Dorothy had hoped that he might come and live with her in Kent. To this end, she asked her husband to accompany her on a visit to Maidstone police station where it might be possible to obtain a permit. The unusual nature of the relationship that still existed between this estranged husband and wife is once again demonstrated by Walter's agreement to this request.

Journeying to Matfield, accompanied by Florence, they visited the police station, but their efforts were to go unrewarded. Generally, the resources of the police were so heavily stretched that they simply could not take responsibility for the additional work involved in keeping an eye on yet one more alien living in the county. In retrospect, the decision does seem a little unfair, especially as Denmark's former neutrality had been blasted to pieces when German troops tore through their common border.

It was less than a fortnight after this joint visit to Maidstone that tragedy struck. On 9 July, with German aircraft carrying out one of their daily attacks upon Channel shipping, eighty-three-year-old John Leury, a cowman from neighbouring Geddes Farm, discovered the bodies of Dorothy and Freda Fisher together with that of their servant, Charlotte Saunders. All three had been brutally murdered. Both mother and daughter had been gunned down in the orchard immediately behind the house, whilst Charlotte had been killed in the kitchen. As if policing the nation's front-line county was not providing sufficient work for an under-manned Kent constabulary, they had now to investigate a horrific triple murder.

Having been notified by John Leury, Special Police Sergeant Harry Crickmay, one of the county's wartime auxiliaries, arrived at Crittenden Cottage shortly after 7p.m. Lacking any real training, for Crickmay was really the village schoolmaster, he made a cursory examination of the house and orchard before calling for assistance. Within two hours, much of the county's detective force was on the scene, with Detective Inspector Francis Smeed from Maidstone eventually taking charge of the local inquiry. A thorough search of the property was undertaken that same evening, with a number of possible clues coming to light.

Most important was the untidy state of the house, the contents of drawers and cupboards haphazardly emptied onto the floor. From this, detectives at the scene of the crime quickly concluded the motive to have been theft. A further clue supporting this conclusion came from the kitchen. At the time of her death Charlotte Saunders appeared to have been carrying a tray of crockery. Leastways the tray, together with a set of smashed cups and saucers, lay near her lifeless body. From this, it could only be concluded that Dorothy and Freda had just finished taking tea outside when the intruder struck. Such a scenario also suggested the events to have occurred in the late afternoon, the earlier part of the day having witnessed a fairly constant drizzle.

If all three women had been in the orchard, the cottage

would have given the appearance of being empty. If the attack had been carried out by an intruder, the police assumed that the murderer had first knocked on the door in order to confirm that the cottage was truly empty. With the knock unheard by those in the orchard, and their being hidden by a screen of trees, the burglar would then have entered the premises with the intention of removing a few valuable items. Whilst in the process of rifling through various cupboards and drawers, the intruder was apparently disturbed by Charlotte Saunders' returning the tray to the kitchen. As likely as not, surprise at seeing an intruder in the kitchen had caused her to drop the tray.

At this point, so the police believed, the burglar attacked Charlotte, beating her about the head with a blunt instrument. Her screams would have brought the other two women back to the house, where they also came upon the burglar. Afraid of being identified at a later stage, the intruder proceeded to chase both women into the orchard, where they were subsequently shot.

That evening an investigation was made into the movement of gypsies and other itinerant travellers who might have been in the area of Matfield that afternoon. It was possible that the killer had this sort of background, and it was necessary to know the names and descriptions of all members of such groups before they moved out of the county. It was also a typical police response, the local constabulary being inclined to associate inexplicable crimes of rural violence with Kent's high gypsy population. An even greater possibility was that the burglar was one of hundreds of soldiers recently brought into mid-Kent to counter the threat of invasion. Again, enquiries at the various army camps would have to be made, there being a distinct possibility that the bullets used were Army issue.

Of one thing Detective Inspector Smeed was certain: his own constabulary did not have the resources to investigate these murders fully. If the various Army camps were to be visited, a great deal of additional personnel would be required. For this reason, contact was made with Scotland Yard, the Chief Constable of Kent seeking immediate assistance.

It was at 11p.m. that Detective Chief Inspector Peter Beveridge, head of the world-famous Flying Squad, first came to hear of the tiny village of Matfield and of the triple murder it had suffered earlier that day. With blackout regulations and various other wartime restrictions, it would not make a great deal of sense for him to travel into Kent that same night. However, he could commence his own investigation by calling upon Dorothy Fisher's Danish lover.

At the time, Westergaart was a definite suspect. In Peter Beveridge's experience, the majority of murders were carried out by those well acquainted with the victim. Perhaps Westergaart and Dorothy had had a lovers' tiff, with things getting out of hand. If this had been the case, the Dane might well have been forced to remove any witnesses. Certainly it was not beyond the realms of possibility.

Arriving at an expensive West End flat, Beveridge and his assistant, Detective Sergeant Tansell, were immediately ushered into a tastefully decorated lounge. As the two officers briefly indicated what had occurred within the grounds of Crittenden Cottage, they carefully watched every expression on Westergaart's face. To all intents and purposes he seemed genuinely shocked and at one time seemed to verge on hysteria. But then he might be a good actor! Preferring to reserve judgement, the two officers chose not to remove him from their short-list of suspects and carried out a thorough search of his flat.

The following morning Beveridge and Tansell made an early start for Bicester. It was their intention to break the news to Walter Fisher – another possible suspect. They arrived shortly after 8a.m., but Walter was already on his way to Aylesbury station. Armed with a brief description of the man, the two Scotland Yard officers intercepted him there. Like Westergaart, he was shocked when told of the tragedy.

Returning to Carramore Farm, the two detectives carried out a brief search of the premises, discovering that Walter Fisher owned several guns. Although none showed signed of recent use, they provided evidence of his ability to use such weapons. As for his claim to have spent the previous day at his London office, this was something that could be checked at a later stage. In the meantime, Walter was asked to accompany the two detectives to Matfield, where he was required to identify the three bodies.

Perhaps the one thing that helped allay any further suspicions as to Walter's being the murderer was the statement he made after examining the discarded contents of the various drawers. In his opinion, nothing seemed to have been taken. If he had carried out the murders, the emptying of these drawers would have been for the purpose of leading the police on a false trail. To this end, he would certainly have encouraged belief in this version of events, listing a few stolen items for good measure.

Something else that police found of interest was the broken crockery. Beveridge had ordered its careful piecing together. To everyone's surprise, it was found to total four cups and four side plates. Was it possible that the murderer had stayed for tea?

Instantly, suspicion once more fell upon Matfield's once frequent visitor, Dorothy's Danish paramour.

Whilst the police continued to examine the cottage and orchard – even prepared to drain a small pond, a host of London journalists began to gather. For them, the tragedy at Matfield was a welcome break from the constant reporting of war news and the need to bolster the morale of an endangered nation.

Amongst the journalists present were a number of accredited war correspondents, many of them already based nearby in order to report on daily events in the battle for Britain. Representing the *Daily Mirror* was Ewart Brooks. Unlike many of his fellow journalists, he had seen actual war service, obtaining a temporary commission when he had taken his motorboat out to Dunkirk to assist in the evacuation. Using his various resources as a reporter, he now managed to obtain a final 'scoop' before being called away to join the Navy on a more permanent basis. This 'scoop' consisted of a short interview with Walter Fisher in which the distraught husband declared that, 'The police and I are completely mystified. I know of no enemy that my wife, daughter or Miss Saunders could have had.'

A more detailed search of the cottage had resulted in several additional discoveries. Most curious, perhaps, was the finding of a white hogskin glove in the orchard close to where Dorothy Fisher had fallen. As no matching glove was discovered, it was thought possible that it might have been left by the murderer.

Exciting additional police interest were several letters found in a writing bureau. Involving three people, named 'Lizzie', 'Julie' and 'Peter', the most interesting was one from 'Julie' denying that she was under any kind of mental strain. Apparently the person signing herself 'Lizzie' had suggested it to 'Peter', explaining that this might be the reason for a series of wild allegations made against Freda. In denying the suggestion, 'Julie' had written to 'Lizzie': 'I am certainly a little worried, but I could not run this place (Carramore Farm) if I were labouring under any mental strain as you suggest, and I can assure you that I am usually very level headed when on a job. I very seldom write letters but when I do they are penned after much thought.' Then, referring specifically to Freda and some sort of outburst she had had during a recent visit to the farm, 'Julie' declared: 'I may be extremely dense, but there seems to be some mystery about the whole situation which I am unable to solve, mystery not being a strong point with me unless in a cheap detective story, so I feel I must withdraw and leave her to you, as her father seems as mystified as I am.'

Upon Walter Fisher's explaining the significance of these letters, the police suddenly became aware of just how complicated his social life had become over the last few years. 'Julie' was, of course, Florence Ransome, whom Beveridge had briefly met at Carramore Farm, when she had been introduced to him as the farm secretary. Now, of course, this revelation made her an additional suspect. As for the other two names mentioned, these were pet-names used by Walter Fisher (who was 'Peter') and Dorothy Fisher (who was 'Lizzie'). Indeed, it appeared that anyone who came into contact with Walter underwent an immediate name-change.

On the following day, Beveridge was again to be found at Piddington, this time interviewing Florence. He took with him the hogskin glove. Arriving a little before midday, he immediately questioned Florence as to her whereabouts on the Tuesday. In replying to this question, she was quite adamant that she had been nowhere near the village of Matfield, indicating that this could be confirmed by Mrs Guildford, one of the farm helpers. Before checking this fact, Beveridge produced the hogskin glove, asking Florence if she recognized it.

'No,' came the very definite response.

'Perhaps you wouldn't mind trying it on.'

'But it looks too small.'

'Nevertheless, if you wouldn't mind trying it on,' Beveridge persisted.

'It is too tight,' she responded as she pulled the glove over her hand. 'I can get it on but it's tight.'

The head of Flying Squad, for his part, considered it to be a perfect fit but chose to say nothing.

Turning his attention to Mrs Guildford, Beveridge was to uncover yet another strange facet of this inquiry. He discovered that she was Florence Ransome's mother. Even stranger to relate, Walter Fisher was totally unaware of this small fact. He was also unaware that Mrs Guildford's son Fred, who also worked on the farm, was Florence's brother. As far as Walter was aware, both Mrs Guildford and Fred were ordinary farmhands whom Florence had employed on the basis of their references.

Far more important from the point of view of the murder inquiry was a statement by Mrs Guildford that she had not seen Florence on the day of the murder. For Beveridge, this was of crucial importance. If Florence had not been on the farm, where had she been?

Going on to question Fred Ransome, they discovered that not only had he given his sister shooting lessons but on the day before the murder she had borrowed his single-loader shotgun together with a dozen cartridges. At the time she had claimed that she was going rabbit-shooting, and she had returned the rifle on the evening of the murder.

The decision to apprehend Florence Ransome for further questioning was taken on the Friday. The continuing police investigations at Matfield had now produced a number of witnesses who had all seen a youngish, auburn-haired woman on the day of the shooting. According to these various witnesses, she was fashionably dressed and had been carrying a long brown-paper parcel. As to where she was going, this was cleared up by the local baker, who admitted that he had given her a lift in his van, taking her to Tonbridge, where she had caught the London train. Perhaps the most noticeable thing about the woman had been her bright red fingernails, a touch of vanity that seemed out of place in wartime rural Kent.

The arrest took place in High Holborn, Chief Inspector

Beveridge having discovered from Walter Fisher that Florence was to be in London, having arranged to meet him outside a solicitor's office. Apparently she was extremely worried about the second police visit to the farm, especially as this had resulted in the removal of her brother's rifle.

As she came into view along the crowded city street, Peter Beveridge stepped forward.

'Mrs Ransome, I believe.'

As he politely raised his bowler hat, a *Daily Express* photographer snapped the moment for posterity. It was an example of how closely the press were following the case. As Florence was brought to Scotland Yard, more photographers clustered around her. Rarely did the newspapers have such a good-looking murderer to grace their front pages. To prevent the course of justice being compromised, however, all the photographers present agreed that their picture would not be published until after an identification parade had been held.

At Tonbridge, on the following Monday, a number of local women, similar in looks to Florence Ransome, were asked to join an identity parade. All were dressed in the blue trousers and colourful top that the woman seen near Matfield had been described as wearing. Despite this uniformity of clothing, none of the witnesses had difficulty in picking out Florence Ransome. A Tonbridge station ticket-collector, a fourteen-year-old charcoal-burner and the baker all agreed that she was the woman they had seen.

The outcome was that Mrs Ransome was formally cautioned by Detective Inspector Smeed on behalf of the Kent County Constabulary. Standing directly in front of her, he informed her that, 'On the night of 9 July at Crittenden, Matfield, I saw the bodies of Dorothy Fisher, Freda Fisher and Charlotte Saunders. As a result of inquiries I am going to charge you with murdering these women.'

'I didn't do it!' she responded. 'I didn't do it! How could I?'

Led away to the cells, she started to scream. 'No! No!' were her only audible words.

The trial, like her arrest, attracted considerable attention. Opening at the Old Bailey during the height of the London Blitz, it was to be the first murder trial in modern history in which the jury, because of the ferocity of the bombing, were allowed to go home each night instead of being locked up in a hotel. Despite the problems created by this aerial bombardment, the trial was relatively unaffected, although the judge, Mr Justice Tucker, had to be ready at a moment's notice to adjourn should the courtroom be threatened by a raid. Ordinary alerts were, however, ignored, 'spotters' located on top of the building giving warning only when bombers were in the immediate vicinity.

Perhaps the most important aspect of the trial was the decision on the part of the prosecution to focus on the overwhelming weight of evidence which suggested the murder to have been premeditated. Of particular significance was the fact that Florence Ransome had spent some of the previous week in learning how to load and fire the small sporting rifle that had belonged to her brother. In addition, she had taken the gun with her, having carefully wrapped it in brown paper. This, if nothing else, proved that the shooting could not have been the result of a sudden aberration.

As further evidence of her single-minded desire to carry out these acts of murder, it was pointed out that not only had she shot Freda and Dorothy whilst they were running away from her but, once they had fallen to the ground, she had fired several times into their lifeless bodies. The subsequent murder of Charlotte Saunders had been conducted not out of malice but simply to help conceal the identity of the murderer. To this same end, Florence had also attempted to leave the house in such a state that the motive would appear to have been that of theft.

The only defence offered by Florence Ransome was that she had no memory of what had happened on the day of the murder. In denying the charge, she told the court that on the day in question she had planned on going to London, where she had an appointment with a doctor.

'I remember standing on the edge of the farm in a field when I saw the 8.27 train – the train I would have caught,' claimed Florence from the witness-box. 'I must have stayed there for a little time because I then saw the 8.56 pass by,' she continued. 'I do not remember what happened afterwards until I went back to bed. The next thing I clearly remember was falling in a field and striking my head.'

Shortly afterwards, during this court appearance, she was handed the empty shotgun and asked about the lessons she had been given on how to fire it.

'I asked my brother for lessons ever since he had the gun,' she told the jury. 'I had tried with Mr Fisher's rifle some years ago to shoot. I was not even able to hold it properly.'

Explaining her loss of memory, Florence claimed that it had been worrying her for a long time. Sometimes it was accompanied by feelings of giddiness, and on other occasions she had found herself wandering in the lane of the farm. None of this, however, could be substantiated.

On Tuesday 12 November 1940, with London still recovering from another night-time air raid, the jury was asked to consider its verdict. After forty-seven minutes of deliberation, they found Florence Ransome guilty of the charge. Having remained perfectly calm throughout the trial, she now drooped her head and visibly shook.

'I am innocent!' were her only words.

Upon the judge's passing a sentence of death, Florence Ransome's composure deserted her completely. Unable to believe what was happening to her, she simply collapsed into the arms of an escorting prison warder. It was to be several minutes before she was revived and in a fit state to be removed from the dock.

In the event, Florence Ransome was never to face the public executioner. Although her appeal failed, she was later certified insane. She was committed to the same Broadmoor asylum in which, almost a hundred years earlier, the Victorian artist Richard Dadd had been housed during his later years of incarceration.

Unexplained, even to this day, is Florence Ransome's motive. Apart from those few brief letters found in the lounge bureau at Crittenden Cottage, it does appear that Florence and Dorothy usually got on extremely well. Nor did she appear to dislike Freda, for in that same batch of letters she endearingly referred to the Fishers' younger daughter as 'Freda, my duck'. Her only complaint about the girl concerned that sudden and subsequently unexplained 'outburst' which occurred whilst Freda was staying at Carramore Farm.

One possibility is that Florence feared that Dorothy and Walter were planning to re-establish the family home on a new basis, with Florence and Westergaart both being abandoned. If Florence had been under some kind of mental strain, such a fear might well have become a fixation which dominated her mind. Despite the existence of a great deal of contrary evidence, Florence may well have interpreted everything in a totally opposite direction, leaving her to believe that the only solution was the destruction of Dorothy.

As for the loss of memory, this may well have been genuine. The human mind can never be so completely callous that the shock of committing a murder is totally ignored. Possibly Florence, although appearing to act both calmly and collectedly, was also suffering an inner repugnance that led to her mind's repressing the memory of the murder and those linked events.

Yet such a suggestion is partially offset by the one

definite lie she is known to have told. In her statement to the jury she said that she saw the 8.56 train from the bottom of one of the farm fields. In no way could she have seen this train. In fact, this was the very train which she is known to have caught to London. For evidence of this, reference must be made to a second identity parade held at Holloway Prison. On this occasion, both the Bicester station master and the train's own ticket-collector agreed that they had seen her actually board this particular train.

Perhaps, if Mrs Ransome had been less good-looking, less concerned about her make-up and less extravagant in her clothing, she might have got away with that triple murder. But it was her striking appearance that forced many a male eye to turn – and, once seen, she was never forgotten. Or, at least, once seen by a man, she was never forgotten, for, of all those witnesses who remember seeing her, not one was female.

– 8 –
The American Way of Death, Chatham, 1951

The townspeople of Chatham witnessed two directly contrasting funerals in the second week of June 1951.

The first, held on Monday 11 June, began with a steady trickle of wreaths to the home of the bereaved family. All were accompanied by either messages of sorrow or references to the sad loss of a popular Chatham resident. From his wife, then confined to hospital and unable to attend the service, came a simple wreath that bore the sadly poignant words, 'Good night darling'.

As the motorcade of one hearse and three Daimlers set out from the small terraced house in Palmerston Road, a great crowd of people lined the streets. They, too, wished to use this opportunity of paying their last respects, some bowing their heads as the cortège slowly headed out of the Medway area and towards the crematorium at Charing. Here a further crowd had assembled, their numbers bolstered by a hundred policeman who had also expressed a desire to be present.

The second Chatham funeral was conducted just one day later. On this occasion there was no motorcade, nor a crowd lining the appropriate streets leading to the town's cemetery. Even within the grounds of the cemetery there was not a single wreath or mourner to be seen. In fact, the funeral, conducted at eight o'clock in the morning, had been kept a deliberate secret. Some may have wished to be present, but their motives were unlikely to be charitable. As like as not, they would have attempted to disrupt the event.

Despite the contrast the funerals were inextricably linked. The first was that of a thirty-three year old police constable, Alan George Baxter, and the second was that of his murderer, twenty-year-old Alan Derek Poole.

On the evening of Monday 5 June, PC Baxter, together with Police Sergeant William Langford and PC Brown, had responded to a 999 phone call. Told of a gunman hiding out in the Luton area of Chatham, they had entered the corporation rubbish dump where, after a brief search, they had found themselves pinned down by a cascade of bullets from an automatic weapon. The unarmed PC Baxter, hit several times, was rushed to St Bartholomew's Hospital, where he died eighteen hours later.

The events leading to PC Baxter's death began a few hours earlier on that same Monday evening in June. Building worker David Tutt and three of his friends were out walking in the countryside not far from the corporation dump when they were confronted by a masked man and two girls. The man, whom they later described as 'rough'-looking, held a Sten gun in the crook of his arm. Moving towards the group of walkers, he pointed the gun at them and shouted, 'Get out, you're yellow!'

The four youths were in no position to argue. Quickly turning round, they ran in the general direction of Sharsted Road. Here, they stopped at one of two farm cottages and explained to the occupant exactly what had taken place. He decided that the best thing to do would be to go and have words with this masked man, a dog being taken as an extra precaution. David Tutt, later recalling these events to a newshound of the *Daily Herald*, said, 'We found the man and the girls, and the man began to fire on us – about 6 to 8 rounds. We dropped on our stomachs. The gunman then turned and ran off with the girls.'

Somewhat shocked by their experience, all five quickly returned to Sharsted Road, where one of them made a 999 emergency call to the police.

At Chatham police station PC Alan Baxter, driver of the Chatham radio-equipped squad car, had just come on duty. An experienced policeman, he had first joined the force in 1938. He took time out during the war to serve in the merchant navy and returned to the Kent Constabulary in 1945. He had recently completed a posting to the Isle of Grain, where he had served as one of the village 'bobbies'. In Chatham, Baxter had seen a more hectic period of service: his pocket notebook bulged with references to cautioned drivers and numerous arrests for drunk-and-disorderly behaviour. Out on the Isle of Grain, with its quiet roads and fairly law-abiding citizenry, matters rarely went further than a sharp rebuke and an occasional warning.

However, his thoughts at that moment were probably directed towards his own personal life. The last few days had proved somewhat harrowing. During the previous week his father had died of a stroke, and he had only just returned from All Saints Hospital where he had been comforting his wife, who had given birth to a stillborn baby. It was their second attempt at adding a child to the family, an earlier pregnancy having ended in a similar fashion.

Upon being notified of that emergency phone call, Baxter headed out towards the car pound accompanied by his sergeant, William Langford, and PC Brown. In those days, the town's police station stood just off New Road, ideally placed for a fast run to Luton. With the forward mounted automatic bell announcing their presence to other road-users, they reached the bottom end of Luton Road within four minutes. Here, at the 'Hen and Chickens', they were waved down by one of the group who had recently been fired upon. Jumping into the squad car, he related the incident and described where it had occurred.

The nearest piece of road to the shooting actually led straight into the corporation rubbish dump. Parking the squad car to one side, Sergeant Langford and PC Brown commenced a search of the area, whilst Baxter remained in the car. The dump was surrounded by a number of huts and old houses, and the two policemen looked there for any signs of unlawful habitation.

At first, the search proved fairly fruitless, but just as Langford was about to suggest looking further afield, he noticed a broken window in one of the huts. Climbing up on some boxes, he peered through the broken glass. Looking into a room below, he could just make out three people who were in the process of opening the hut door. Forgetting that one of them was armed, Langford rushed round to the front of the building with the intention of apprehending them. As he came within twenty yards of the fleeing figures, the man holding the gun suddenly stopped and turned round. Pointing the Sten gun at Sergeant Langford, he showed every intention of firing.

'Don't be a bloody fool!' Langford shouted.

But it had no effect. All the sergeant heard in reply was a yell he couldn't make out and the staccato sound of an automatic gun unloading its deadly missiles. Fortunately, the gunman was fairly inexperienced, failing to take into account that a gun of this calibre has a tendency to pull to the left. The burst of bullets being fired missed Langford by a yard or more.

Realizing that the gunman was probably serious in his attempts to wound or kill him, Langford turned and ran. With darkness now falling, he failed to see a pile of barbed wire, tripped and fell to the ground. The young man who had accompanied the three officers and had been helping in searching the huts thought Langford had been hit. On seeing him pull himself up and take cover, he felt a distinct sense of relief.

But such feelings were to prove ill-founded and short-lived.

The gunman now headed for the squad car, where PC Baxter was still seated. Again the would-be killer pulled the trigger of the gun. Another stream of bullets flew out, catching the windscreen and shattering it with hideous bang. Baxter, recovering from the shock, pushed open the door and drew out his truncheon. But he stood not a chance. The gunman fired yet again. This time the bullets found their mark as Police Constable Alan Baxter fell to the ground.

Having done his worst, the gunman jumped over a gate and disappeared. By this time, the girls had also vanished.

First to reach the stricken man was Sergeant Langford. But already, it would appear, Baxter realized that he had been hit too badly to be saved.

'He's got me in the guts, Sarge. I've had it,' he whispered. 'I'm going.'

'No you're not, son. You'll be all right,' Langford reassured him. 'Let's see what the damage is.'

But as Langford loosened the man's collar, he realized just how little hope there was. Despite having been shot only moments earlier, Baxter was already covered in blood. His only chance was immediate hospital treatment. Carefully placing him in the back of the squad car, Langford drove the vehicle directly to the accident unit at St Bartholomew's Hospital. Four hours later PC Baxter underwent an emergency operation, but overall doctors felt that there was little that could could be done for him. In the morning a statement was issued that declared him to be 'extremely poor and serious'.

With Baxter's life slowly ebbing away, a massive search of the Medway area was soon under way. The police knew little or nothing about the man they sought. All they were able to do was release a very brief description. It was estimated that he was aged about twenty and had been wearing blue clothes and a roll-neck sweater. Apart from his being armed with a Sten gun, it was also said that he was carrying a sheath-knife.

Overnight a careful watch was kept on the open ground that surrounded Luton, with armed police located around an eighteen-square-mile area. In the towns of Chatham, Gillingham and Rochester a number of road-blocks were established, all cars and lorries being stopped and checked.

At first light the search was intensified. Hundreds of soldiers and sailors were drafted in from several of the local barracks. They joined the police in a co-ordinated search of a large triangular area of open countryside and woodland between Luton to the north, Blue Bell Hill to the south-west and Wigmore to the south-east. Nowadays, of course, much of this land has been claimed for housing, but in those days it included the extensively wooded area of Walderslade.

Forming themselves into a loosely spaced ring, soldiers, sailors and police gradually converged on an area somewhere towards the centre. Should anyone still be hiding in this area, they would certainly be found. A warning was given to the servicemen: under no circumstances were they to tackle or fire upon the gunman should he be found; this was to be left to the police. Although the police were prepared to shoot him, it was hoped that the gunman would give himself up peacefully.

It was not long before the search bore results. Although the gunman himself was not found, his two female companions were soon caught. Taken to Chatham police station for questioning, it turned out that they had both escaped from a remand home in Gloucester. One of them, a seventeen-year-old, told the police that she had known the gunman for two years. He was an Army deserter whom she named as Alan Poole. Apparently he had been a member of the Royal Corps of Signals and had gone absent without leave. Amongst the items he took with him were a Sten gun and a considerable amount of ammunition. The girl also said that Poole was local to Chatham, his parents living in Symons Avenue, on a council estate within a mile of where PC Baxter had been shot.

The police further learnt that since Poole had deserted he had been living in the open, stealing food or purchasing it from local gypsies. The girls had been involved in some of these thefts, with one of them helping Poole break into a local factory canteen from which they had stolen several tins of meat, swiss rolls and chocolate.

Neither of the girls really knew why he had attacked the four youths who had approached them on Monday night, although it was probable that he was just showing off. Having used the gun once, he had said to the girls that if the police came he was prepared to shoot it out with them. He seemed quite fearless.

On the afternoon of the day on which PC Baxter died, his wife, knowing of his serious situation, was brought by ambulance from All Saints Hospital. Her own condition, although slowly improving, meant that she had to lie down, and she was allowed the use of a hospital operating trolley. Seeing her there as he temporarily regained consciousness, Baxter told his wife, 'I think I've had it.' As Peggy leaned over to kiss him, doctors and nurses, who knew there was little chance, looked away.

The police, now aware of exactly whom they were looking for, had a distinctly easier task before them. Indeed, a quick glance through their own criminal record files revealed that not only had they got Poole on their 'wanted' list, following his desertion from the Army in October, but he was a known offender who had been arrested on several earlier occasions.

His first clash with the police had taken place in 1946, when he had been committed to the West Kent Quarter Sessions for a total of nineteen office-breaking offences. Sent to an approved school, he had absconded, returning to Chatham, where he was again in trouble with the police when he broke into a sports pavilion. He was sentenced to three years' Borstal training, then a further escape resulted in a short interlude of breaking into shops prior to his arrest and return to Borstal.

Over the years Poole seemed to develop a deep hatred of the police, these feelings reaching a temporary peak during April 1949 when he again absconded. It was in that month that he first attacked a police officer, threatening a Chatham constable with a knife. As with his two previous escapes, the outcome was his return to Borstal for further punishment.

It seems that the motivating force in Alan Poole's life was that of American gangster comics and films. Always he appeared to model himself on the anti-heroes of the gangland underworld. According to a neighbour in Symons Avenue, 'Poole looked like a gangster. He walked like a gangster. He talked out of the side of his mouth like a gangster.' Furthermore, as this same neighbour also indicated, Poole 'died like a gangster'!

Apart from a few clothes, the Sten gun and a knife, Poole took very few personal possessions into hiding with him. However, one thing that was discovered during the all-day search of the Sharsted area was a box of American comics. Whilst he could do without other luxuries, such essential reading could not be abandoned. He seemed to imagine himself as a British Al Capone, or judging by the way he freely sacrificed his own life in a totally one-sided shoot out, as a character from the film *White Heat*, a fictional gangster who had ended his life in similar circumstances. The film was shown at Chatham towards the end of the previous year, and one assumes that Poole may have been amongst the hundreds who queued to see this box-office hit, which starred James Cagney in the memorable role of Cody Jarrett.

Aware that Poole would have to find another hiding-place, the police felt it more than possible that he might attempt to seek sustenance from his parents at 114 Symons Avenue. For this reason a number of armed police were discreetly placed around the Pooles' house, their instructions being either to arrest Poole or to seek reinforcements if he should turn up. Remaining in position throughout the night, there was at first nothing to report. However, things began to happen early that following morning. First it was the mundane. At around 8a.m. Albert Poole, Alan's father, returned from night-shift work. A little later Doreen Poole, Derek's eleven-year-old sister left for school and then unexpectedly returned. Finally, a little after 9a.m. they saw Mrs Poole and Doreen hurriedly leaving the front of the house, whilst from the back there was the distinctive sound of Sten gun fire echoing through the entire council estate. Poole was already in the house and, for some reason, was firing the Sten gun from the rear window.

The event which appears to have sparked Poole's desire finally to shoot it out seems to have been Doreen's return from school. On entering the house, she was clearly very upset.

'Oh Mummy, I have been sent home from school,' she sobbed. 'The girls are laughing at me and saying that Alan shot a policeman.'

Mrs Poole, herself close to tears, sat down and started writing a note to Doreen's teacher. At that point Alan Poole, who had been in the attic, burst into the room.

'Don't write a word!' he shouted. 'Get your hats and

coats on and get out. I'm going to shoot it out with the cops.'

Terrified by what her son had said, Mrs Poole went into the other room to get her husband. Apparently he was still unaware of Alan's presence in the house, having been out since the previous afternoon.

'Good God, son, where have you been?' he asked in amazement. 'You know the police want you!'

'I'm going to shoot it out with them,' and then with words that could have come straight out of a script for *White Heat* or any one of a dozen similar films: 'They'll never take me alive. I've plenty of ammunition and I'm going to kill some more of the bastards!'

Without any attempt to talk him out of it, Alan Poole finally turned to Doreen. Using words that could again have come from an American film script, he finally declared, 'Goodbye. You won't see me again.'

Mrs Poole beckoned Doreen towards the front door, whilst she herself grabbed hold of a younger son who was not yet of school age. Albert Poole, however, still wishing to remonstrate with his son, stayed a moment longer but he could see from the crazed look on his son's face that it would have no effect. Leaving by the rear door, he made his way along the back gardens. When he was no more than fifty yards from the house, Alan Poole opened fire. Deliberately shooting high, he was, nevertheless, aiming in the general direction of his father. It was both a threat to the older man and a pointless 'come and get me' gesture.

It was the sound of these shots being fired that caught the attention of the armed police already positioned close to the house. Knowing that their quarry was now cornered, one or two of them moved forward in the hope that he might give himself up. By now, Alan Poole had moved to a front upstairs bedroom which it appears he had previously prepared by up-ending a bed to use as a barricade. Looking out of the window, he saw this movement going on below him and proceeded to open fire. Those caught out in the open dived for cover, whilst others returned the fire with their own single-shot .303 rifles.

As news spread that PC Baxter's killer was in Symons Avenue, police reinforcements began to arrive, a number of them also armed. At the same time, further support was given by the Army and Navy, with large detachments of military personnel also on hand. Whilst some of the armed police took up position within range of the Pooles' house, other groups of police officers began to evacuate neighbouring houses that were likely to be struck by stray bullets.

With each passing minute it became increasingly obvious not only that Poole was unlikely to surrender but that he fully intended killing another policeman. Every so often he would unleash a further round of bullets, aimed at the countless numbers of uniformed officers sheltering behind garden walls and old air-raid shelters. Following each indiscriminate firing of the Sten gun, there was a similar burst of fire from a ring of armed snipers.

As one London newspaper commented, it was reminiscent of the famous siege of Sydney Street. With over 200 soldiers eventually brought to Symons Avenue, combined with the large number of armed police, it could equally have been described as a re-enactment of a World War II fire-fight in some distant European town.

Unable to bring Poole to his senses, other tactics were eventually adopted. It was decided that tear-gas grenades should be used. A small stock had already been acquired from one of the barracks, with a former colour sergeant agreeing to run the gauntlet of Poole's erratic firing and lob a couple of them into the house. Because of the risk of one of these exploding grenades causing a sudden blaze, the fire brigade were also brought in, a number of hoses simultaneously pumping water into the house.

Following the explosion of the grenades, all that could be heard from inside 114 Symons Avenue was the firing of the Sten gun. As on previous occasions, it resulted in a series of return shots from the armed police officers. Then everything went silent.

It was a silence that was to last nearly two hours.

As family and neighbours awaited further developments, some of the journalists who had assembled began to search out likely people to interview. Most sought-after were Albert and Dorothy Poole. A *Daily Herald* reporter managed to get Albert talking. His interview appeared in the following day's newspaper. 'Alan', so Albert Poole was recorded as saying, 'was always the bad one of the family – the only one of my ten children who has given me and my wife any trouble. We could do nothing with him.'

Presumably, as the interview continued, Albert Poole and the *Herald* journalist also received the occasional whiff of tear-gas. By this time it was covering much of the street. But it did not seem to stop Alan Poole's father from continuing his monologue. 'He was born at Luton and went to the village school. But he was never like the other boys. He was not interested in games, but spent his spare time wandering in the woodlands. Later he became crazy about knives and weapons. He always carried some sort of knife which he kept sharpening. His only reading was American detective and gangster magazines. He was a bad boy and I say that even though I was his father.'

The *Daily Mail* carried an interview with Dorothy Poole. She reiterated a number of the points previously made by her husband. In concluding the interview, which mentioned his desertion from the Army and events that had taken place earlier in the day, she simply said, 'Ever since he was a lad he has caused me quite a lot of trouble.'

As the journalists began writing up their stories, the final scene began to unfold. A party of police officers, led by Chatham's Chief Superintendent C. F. Broughton, broke open the front door and rushed into the house, their guns at the ready. With fears of a possible massacre at the forefront of most people's thoughts, the assembled crowd nervously awaited the sound of gunfire. Instead, all that occurred was the waving of a white handkerchief from the upper front window. It was Broughton indicating that it was all over. The killer of PC Baxter was dead. He had not taken his own life, as many had thought possible, but had been killed during that last fusillade of return fire.

The man who had chosen to live by the gun had died by the gun. Influenced by those American comics and gangster movies, Alan Derek Poole had chosen to die in the fashion of his heroes. As one further national newspaper stated, the American way of death had come to Chatham on that sunny June morning in 1951.

– 9 –
A Small Village Affair,
Aldington,
1961

Early on the morning of Saturday 13 May 1961 David Pilcher, a milk-roundsman in the village of Aldington, came upon a sight he would never forget. As he approached the porch of Pantiles Cottage, where he placed two pints each morning, he saw the semi-clad body of the thirty-eight-year-old woman he knew as Alice Buxton, one of the occupants of this isolated cottage that stands a little to the east of the main village. It was clear that she had met a terrible and unnatural end. She was dressed only in a pink slip and cardigan, and her head was bloodied and mutilated.

The local village 'bobby', PC Allen, having been contacted by Pilcher, was on the scene within minutes. Confirming that Alice Buxton had been killed, he considered it more than likely that she had been shot. Certainly the evidence of the head wound strongly suggested that this was how Alice had met her fate, and the fore-end part of a double-barrelled shot gun that lay by her side strengthened this conclusion.

Carrying out a quick search of the rest of the house, PC Allen entered the scullery. Now it was his turn to come across the unexpected. Lying on the floor, also partly dressed, was the body of Hubert Roderick Buxton, the other occupant of the cottage. Judging by his battered head, he also appeared to have received a direct blast from that same shotgun, part of which lay in the porch. Shortly before 8a.m., therefore, PC Allen sent a hasty message to the main police station at Ashford, where members of the CID were alerted to the double murder.

The Buxtons were relative newcomers to the village of Aldington, having moved into the area two years earlier. Hubert Buxton, a gardener by trade, was employed by Gladys Etta de Pomeroy of nearby Pantiles House, In fact, the bungalow in which the couple had been living belonged to Gladys de Pomeroy and was reserved for use by the gardener and his family. For a time, also, Alice Buxton had been employed by Miss de Pomeroy, working as a maid in the house. More recently, though, she had found employment as a waitress in a Folkestone hotel.

For most of those who knew the Buxtons, the two showed all the outward signs of a happily married couple. Those who made such an assumption were wrong on two counts.

First, although the Buxtons lived as man and wife, they were not really married. Alice Buxton had, some years earlier, upped and left her legal husband and run off with Hubert Buxton, one of her husband's business associates.

Secondly, many would have been mistaken concerning the happiness of the couple. It appears that Hubert was a very difficult person to live with, giving his 'wife' little individual freedom. Apart from the needs of her paid employment, she was rarely allowed out on her own, and he objected to her frequent visits to her mother in Belgium. In fact, Alice was still a Belgian national, with many of her own friends and relatives living in that country. Worse still, from the point of view of their 'common law' marriage, the Buxtons rarely made love, Hubert blaming it on Alice, whom he accused of being frigid.

All this was, of course, between the Buxtons themselves and, unless they had killed each other, appeared to have little bearing upon the circumstances of the double murder. Instead, detectives at the bungalow concluded that they were looking for a late-night intruder who had probably been caught in the act of rifling through some of the Buxtons' valuables, shooting both Hubert and Alice in an effort to escape. Either that or the motive was sexual. Alice, from the position in which she lay on the porch floor, looked very much like a rape victim. Her pink slip was pulled up to her thighs, and one breast was exposed.

Later that afternoon police had to modify some of these earlier theories. After a post mortem carried out by the eminent London pathologist Francis Camps, two interesting observations were brought to their attention. From a careful study of Alice's body, Camps concluded that she had been neither shot nor sexually assaulted. Instead, the murderer had repeatedly smashed a blunt instrument into her head. Possibly, judging by the violence used, the murder might have been carried out by someone who had a considerable grudge against her. On the other hand, Camps did confirm that Hubert Buxton had been shot, the gun probably fired from outside the scullery window.

With an inquiry already under way, the search had to be extended over a wider area. Although the original belief in theft as a possible motive could not be completely ruled out, a number of other factors had to be taken into consideration. Was is possible that the couple had an enemy living either in Aldington, or, maybe, further afield?

One person who had to be eliminated from their inquiries was Alice's legal husband. He had clear grounds for disliking the couple, and it was not impossible that this had led to the violent attack. In the event, however, the husband was eliminated within hours, when it was discovered that he had emigrated to Canada four years earlier. A further possibility was that of a Belgian link. It was not beyond the realms of possibility that the reason for Alice's frequent trips abroad was not so much to visit her mother as to meet a secret lover. Should this be the case, it might also be possible that they had fallen out, this man deliberately travelling to Aldington in order to avenge some perceived slight. For this reason, the Belgian police were notified of the murder and asked to carry out their own inquiries.

The news of this tragic event at Aldington was duly conveyed to all local police officers reporting for duty on that Saturday morning. If for no other reason, those involved in motor-patrol duties would have to be told to use their radios only on channel one. Channel two, which might normally be available to them, had been allocated to the Aldington murder inquiry.

Amongst those receiving the news of the double murder at this time was PC Fred Brisley. He was stationed at Seabrook as the driver of a traffic-division Austin Westminster; his 'patch' took in Folkestone, Hythe and parts of the Romney Marsh as far as the Canterbury end of Stone Street. Having reported for duty at 8a.m., PC Brisley remembers most of that day to have been fairly routine. As always, he had been directed to keep an eye open for traffic offences, defective vehicles and vehicles that he considered to be driven recklessly. At around 10a.m. he decided to take a short break, pulling over to the side of the road. Out of general curiosity he temporarily re-tuned his radio to channel two. It would be interesting to hear whether any progress had been made in the murder inquiry.

As PC Brisley sat there listening, he was rather startled to hear the name Neimasz mentioned over the air. It was an unusual name and one that he was sure he had come across, but where and when he could not remember. For much of the rest of the day his thoughts kept returning to that name. Neimasz, where had he come across it before? Then it came to him. Of course, he was the man who had offered him a cup of tea in a quarry. But he had hardly been dressed for it! Fred Brisley chuckled to himself as he remembered the incident. It had occurred about seven months earlier in a quarry at Hampton Hill near Hythe.

With that day's duty concluded at 4p.m., PC Brisley decided to check one of his old pocket notebooks. He was in the habit of writing everything down; it saved unnecessary complications later on. As he flicked through the pages, he came across the incident he was looking for. It had taken place on 29 September the previous year. The quarry was one he frequently visited. A colleague of his kept bees there, and Brisley was in the habit of breaking the day's duty by calling in for a cup of tea. On that occasion his friend had not been there, but the quarry was occupied. At the end of the road he could see a car half covered with a sheet of tarpaulin. It had not been there half an hour earlier when he had last passed that way.

Although it was not unusual for cars to be in the quarry, the tarpaulin covering made this one look very suspicious. Brisley decided to investigate. As he approached on foot, he could see that the car was moving on its suspension, whilst there were noises coming from inside. As he lifted the tarpaulin everything became clear. Inside he could see a man and a woman who were intent upon enjoying each other's company. They had disarranged clothes, with the woman's blouse undone and her skirt pulled up. Both appeared embarrassed by Brisley's untimely arrival.

'What are you doing?' Brisley enquired of the thick-set, dark-haired man, who was about fifty years of age. It was not that Brisley was naïve: he just needed something to say.

'We are having some tea!' explained the man, who spoke with a heavy foreign accent. To prove the point, he produced a flask. Waving it in the air, it looked very much as if he was offering some to the police constable. The woman, a good-looking brunette whom Brisley later described as having a round face and small features, hastily adjusted her clothing. Although the policeman could have made things difficult for the couple, he decided to let them finish their 'tea' in peace.

'Carry on the good work,' he remarked. 'Oh! And what's your name?'

'Neimasz,' the man replied.

Returning to the police car, Brisley copied down the main points of the encounter. He noted the man's name, incorrectly spelling it as 'Neimaz', the way it had been pronounced. In addition, he noted some points about the car. It was a light grey Hillman Husky with the Kent registration number YKR 866. Finally he added the time. It was 4.45p.m.

Although he considered this incident as probably having no bearing on the murder inquiry, he decided that he should nevertheless draw it to the attention of detectives investigating the case. He made a point of going down to the on-site murder caravan and having a brief word with Detective Inspector Bailey. He was told, however, that, although Neimasz' name had been broadcast, it was only a minor matter involving the discovery of a receipt found in the cottage. For the time being, Brisley thought no more of it.

A few days later Brisley received a phone call at Seabrook police station. It was from Detective Superintendent John du Rose of New Scotland Yard, who was now heading the Aldington inquiry.

In those days it was normal for Scotland Yard officers to be involved in a murder inquiry conducted in Kent. The local constabulary was not really in a position to handle major investigations, calling upon the help of the Yard if an arrest had not been made in forty-eight hours. In more recent years, of course, this has totally changed, the county police easily matching the resources of most other police forces in the country.

Apparently Brisley's earlier conversation with DI Bailey had been duly recorded, and du Rose wanted to know more about the incident. In particular, du Rose wished to know if Brisley would recognize the woman he had seen with Neimasz. Upon Brisley's answering in the affirmative, du Rose asked him if he would be prepared to look at the body of Alice Buxton to see if she was the woman he had seen.

Attending the mortuary at Herne Bay, this being the only refrigerated mortuary in the county, Brisley was confronted by the ghastly sight of both murder victims. First he was shown Alice Buxton, lying naked under a white sheet. The covering was slowly rolled back. The sight was gruesome. Her bruised and bludgeoned head gave every appearance of a gunshot wound. As to her identity, there could be no mistake. This, Brisley confirmed, was the woman he had seen with Neimasz on that day in September.

Du Rose seemed pleased with the findings; and well he might. The murder inquiry was about to be concluded. Brisley had supplied the final link in a chain that now connected Neimasz with both murder victims.

Hendryk Neimasz had, in fact, been interviewed by detectives investigating the double murder within only a few hours of its being reported. Amongst bits and pieces found inside the bungalow was a letter torn into tiny shreds. Although part of the letter was missing, it had been addressed to Alice and signed by Hendryk. A number of kisses had been added.

The Neimaszes had known the Buxton family for about a year. This friendship had began when Alice had met Grypa, Hendryk's wife, on the early morning bus into Hythe. As both women were regular travellers on this bus, it was not long before a genuine friendship had developed. In time, Alice invited Grypa to tea at the bungalow, suggesting that she also bring her husband. This seems to have been the first time Hendryk and Alice met. Later, so it would appear, they started to arrange a series of clandestine meetings, with Hendryk choosing to show Alice the delights of the stone quarry at Hampton Hill. In order that the suspicions of her jealous husband should not be aroused, Alice always ensured that these meetings took place immediately after she had finished work at Hythe, Hendryk driving her back to Aldington so that she arrived at about the same time as the bus she would normally catch.

Hendryk Neimasz was of Polish nationality and spoke surprisingly little English for someone who had lived in Britain for about fifteen years. He had come to Britain shortly after the war, hoping to make a fresh start to his life. During the war he had briefly served in a Polish cavalry regiment before his capture by the Germans and subsequent dispatch to a Brunswick slave-labour camp. In forced employment in a sugar factory, he met the twenty-two-year-old Grypa. She was of Ukrainian nationality, her home having been destroyed as a result of the German invasion of the Soviet Union. After the war both had made their separate ways to Britain, where they eventually started a small family. Through perseverance and hard work, they finally reached a stage where Hendryk could confidently borrow £1,000 to acquire a twenty-acre smallholding in the village of Ham Street. This initial venture into the realms of private enterprise proved highly successful, with Hendryk selling the property at a profit and paying off the loan.

Moving to a cottage in Mersham, a village only three miles from Aldington, Hendryk purchased a second smallholding. This proved less successful than his first venture, and he was eventually forced to take a full-time job. At the time of the murder inquiry he was working as a labourer, employed upon construction of a bridge at Rochester that would eventually take the M2 over the River Medway. Because of the distances involved, he found it necessary to spend most of his weekday evenings in the Medway area, renting a room in Gillingham.

During that first interview with the police, Hendryk claimed that the torn and discarded letter which had been discovered in Pantiles Cottage was of absolutely no importance. It had been written to Alice whilst she was in Belgium and was, he claimed, merely a request for her to indicate the time she would be returning to Dover. According to Hendryk, it had been agreed that he should meet her at Dover. The letter, incidentally, had never reached her in Belgium, Alice having left her mother's home by the time it arrived. Instead it had been forwarded and delivered to the bungalow on the morning of the murder. As for the addition of kisses at the end of the letter, Hendryk explained, in his broken English, 'Missus put kisses, Alice put kisses, I put kisses.'

At the time, the police had taken no further action. Du Rose, however, decided upon a more thorough investigation of Hendryk Neimasz. Having been informed of what PC Brisley had seen, he ordered a search of Hendryk's house and smallholding at Mersham.

This proved decisive, the search uncovering two vital pieces of evidence. First to be found was a bloodstained bicycle, followed by the uncovering of the barrel and stock of a double-barrelled shotgun. This later proved to be part of the gun already found at the site of the crime. Forensic evidence also revealed that the newly found parts to the gun showed traces of human blood, whilst a fingerprint belonging to Hendryk was found on the stock.

Taken in for questioning and told of the mounting evidence against him, Hendryk went some way towards making a full confession. He admitted that a relationship had developed between himself and Alice, but indicated that he had become worried by some of the suggestions she had made. According to Hendryk, Alice had told him that he should kill Grypa, so giving him the freedom to start a new life with her. Such talk, so he claimed, had greatly worried him, and he had eventually thought it possible that Alice herself would kill Grypa and his children.

For some reason, Hendryk had explained these fears to 'George', a man he claimed to have met in a pub near his Gillingham lodgings. This man had agreed to solve Hendryk's problems by killing Alice in 'a non-violent way'. To help George carry out this task, Hendryk said that he had shown him the bungalow where Alice lived. He also claimed to have paid George the sum of £60. According to Hendryk, therefore, it must have been George who had killed the Buxtons on the night of 13 May.

When told that he was to be formally charged with the double murder, Hendryk stuck to this original story. 'I no kill her,' he declared. 'I paid man £60 to kill Alice. I not angry with Roderick.'

With the charge read out to him, Hendryk was asked if he understood.

'You say like I charged twice?' he asked. 'One for Alice and one for Roderick. I still say I do not know what happen. I still say I not kill.'

Despite Hendryk's highly unlikely declarations concerning the mysterious George, the police carried out an extensive investigation in the Gillingham area. But they failed to come up with any evidence to support the man's existence. The inevitable conclusion was drawn: George was a mere fabrication. Besides which, even if he had existed, the evidence still pointed to Hendryk's being the actual killer. Apart from his fingerprints being found on the gun, a subsequent search of his Gillingham room had uncovered a bloodstained pair of cord trousers.

Piecing together information from two eye-witnesses who had been in the area of the Pantiles Bungalow on the night of the murder, it appears that Hendryk had made two visits to the Buxtons. On the first occasion, about 10p.m., his car was seen parked near the cottage. Possibly he had gone to see the Buxtons whilst he was on his way home from Gillingham. He had, however, chosen a rather inopportune moment. The arrival of the letter from Belgium, which was in fact a love-letter to Alice, had fallen into the hands of Hubert Buxton. Far from amused at this discovery, it is likely that he had turned on the amorous Pole.

Alice, for her part, not wishing to lose Hubert, may well have told Hendryk that she did not wish to see him again. Exactly what happened on that first visit will never be known, but the outcome was Hendryk's return to the cottage about an hour later. This time he seems to have used his bicycle, for a second witness saw a cyclist approach the cottage at about 11p.m.

Armed with a loaded shotgun, Hendryk had determined upon killing both Hubert and Alice. His motive is unclear but must have sprung from those harsh words spoken on his first visit. Firing at Hubert through the scullery window, he then attacked Alice. At the time she was preparing for bed and must have rushed out of the house when she heard the shot and been caught by Hendryk in the porch. Smashing the gun down on her head, he continued to hit her whilst she was still on the floor. Later, returning to the village of Mersham, he seems to have retired to his own bed at about 11.30p.m.

In court, Hendryk stuck religiously to his original version of events. When he was brought before the Ashford magistrates for remand prior to the later committal proceedings, the clerk of the court asked him if he had any questions.

'Can I say something now?' he asked.

'You may,' the clerk replied.

'I was in the Army,' Hendryk began. 'I no kill anybody. But this time I was fright for my wife and my family. Otherwise if I had not man to hold me back wife would be killed and two children killed.'

As with all trials that involved heavily publicized murders, the courtroom was packed. Journalists from both local and national newspapers hastily scribbled down his prepared statement, and the few members of the public who had managed to enter the court listened with keen interest.

'The little one was Christian mother to her,' continued Hendryk, who was trying to explain that Alice was the godmother of his youngest child. 'She had gun. She showed me guns. But not this time. Once before when she came from Belgium.'

'I don't want to stop you,' interrupted the clerk of the court, 'but there is no reason why you should make a statement at this stage.'

'I say nothing then,' replied Hendryk with an air of finality.

Hendryk Neimasz was eventually tried at the Lewes Assize Court held in July 1961. To the end he continued to make a number of uncorroborated statements against Alice Buxton, with the judge feeling it necessary to defend her name against these accusations. In addition, Hendryk maintained that it was George who must have carried out the killings, a fact that the jury chose to disregard. The outcome, therefore, was a verdict of guilty on both counts, and Hendryk was sentenced to death. A subsequent appeal was dismissed, and the execution was carried out at Wandsworth prison on 8 September that same year.

– 10 –
An Upward Trend,
Kent,
1980s

Dale Street, Chatham. 4 August 1986. Paddy Kirwan, a wheelchair-bound invalid, fails to answer his front door. It is nine o'clock in the morning, and the person trying to attract his attention is the driver of a Social Services mini-bus. It is a routine visit, the driver regularly collecting Kirwan and taking him to the Shaws Wood Day Centre in Strood.

Unable to get any response from the occupant of the house and knowing that a key is kept just inside the letter-box, the driver decides to let himself in. He is accompanied by a young female social worker whose task is to look after the small number of passengers who join the bus each day. As the driver enters the kitchen, the reason for Kirwan's failure to answer the door becomes immediately apparent. Paddy Kirwan is dead. His body lies slumped in a pool of blood.

It is clear to the driver that there is little that can be done for Kirwan, but he can save the feelings of his young assistant. So that she does not have to witness the horrific sight, he quickly ushers her out of the house before calling the emergency services.

Although the circumstances look suspicious, it is not

until a Home Office pathologist has completed a post mortem that a full-scale murder inquiry can be mounted. After all, it would be wrong to set up a 'hue and cry' if Kirwan had merely collapsed and smashed his head on the side of a table. But, with the post mortem completed that same day, those original suspicions are confirmed. Paddy Kirwan had been unlawfully killed. The Kent constabulary have a murder inquiry on their hands.

As it happens, this particular crime was to be solved in a relatively short period of time. The perpetrator of the terrible act had left a number of clues that would inevitably lead to his capture. Most important were bloodstained fingerprints that had been left both under and over the kitchen work surfaces.

The first officers to arrive at the scene of the crime had merely taken responsibility for searching the house, making sure that nothing was moved nor any evidence destroyed. Amongst others who quickly joined them were members of the police specialist photographic department and fingerprint bureau. Working closely with one another, it was their task to carry out a minute survey of the premises, highlighting and photographing any fingerprints that might possibly relate to Kirwan's death.

The significance of the bloodstained prints in the kitchen, a sequence from the left hand and a right palm print found on the wall, was immediately apparent. Should it be discovered that they did not belong to Paddy Kirwan, it was clear that they were those of his killer or belonged to someone else who was present at the time.

The successful matching of these prints was to lead to the subsequent arrest of one of Kirwan's acquaintances from the Shaws Wood Day Centre. This man, who had a drink problem and was trying to obtain £10, had used the key, which he also knew to be placed just inside the letter-box, to obtain his uninvited entrance into the house. First he had asked Kirwan if he could borrow the money but, in his desperation for alcohol, had become more persistent. Kirwan, never one to hide his feelings, had responded to these repeated requests by hitting the man with his walking-stick. A general fight had ensued in which Kirwan had been mercilessly beaten about the head. It was during this frenzied response to Kirwan's initial attack that the bloodstained fingermarks had been left in various parts of the kitchen.

Of course, the existence of these fingermarks, in themselves, could not possibly have resulted in an arrest had not police already got these same prints on their central file held at Maidstone. Only a few months earlier the man responsible for the death of Paddy Kirwan had been sentenced for shoplifting, and he was actually engaged in a period of community service at the Shaws Wood Centre. As in the case of all convicted criminals, his prints had been taken and duly filed. In the words of one of those involved in this investigation, it only took ten minutes to name the guilty man.

In the event, although police had designated this a murder inquiry, the man brought to trial was subsequently convicted of manslaughter. Receiving an eight-year sentence, the attacker had not been deemed totally responsible for his actions.

Another inquiry that hinged upon the importance of fingerprints occurred in Swanley following the death of Cicely Landless in May 1987. She was found collapsed next to a cupboard, and it was at first thought that she had died from natural causes. Only after a post mortem, when it was revealed that the ninety-year-old widow had a broken bone in her neck, did the county police have cause to suspect she had been murdered.

A thorough search was made of her spacious detached house, but no signs were found either of a break-in or of any of her valuable antiques having been taken. However, it was discovered that her purse was missing. As with all such inquiries, the house was dusted for fingerprints, and the vast majority of marks were soon eliminated as being those either of the victim or of the gardener who had discovered the body. However, one set of prints did not appear to belong to anyone with legitimate access to the house.

Whilst Mrs Landless' home was being searched, teams of detectives were contacting and interviewing anyone known to have visited the house over the past few months. This, quite naturally, included neighbours, tradesmen and friends. In the course of their inquiries, detectives also interviewed her former milkman. Driven to a police station for questioning, he surprised the accompanying officers by making a full confession to the murder, saying that it had occurred as the result of an earlier argument he had had with his girlfriend. That this former milkman was Mrs Landless' killer was subsequently confirmed when his fingerprints were found to match those already discovered at the scene of the crime.

Those investigations carried out by the police at Chatham and Swanley clearly emphasize the continuing importance of fingerprints in a designated murder inquiry. Since the conviction of the Stratton brothers in 1905, all such inquiries have involved an attempt to collect fingerprint evidence, with a variety of techniques evolved for the purpose of highlighting marks from a range of different materials. One recent breakthrough is the development of a metal deposition machine that can be used to develop prints from plastic and polythene.

However, despite the undoubted advances being made in fingerprinting techniques and other areas of forensic science, not all serious crimes are solved as quickly as those so far mentioned. In fact, a very small number of murders committed in Kent over the past ten years have yet to be solved. Amongst these are two particularly vicious murders committed in Tunbridge Wells during 1987.

Although there is no definite evidence that the two murders are linked, there are sufficient similarities to suggest that the murderer may be one and the same person. Both victims, Caroline Pierce and Wendy Knell, lived alone in bed-sit accommodation and died from head wounds following sexual assault. In addition, the two women were both in their twenties and managed a shop and restaurant respectively that were no more than 400 yards distant from one another.

So far, police have expended thousands of hours in their search for the murderer or murderers, using all the facilities at their disposal. In particular, the two murders have been deliberately brought to the attention of the media, it being hoped that there might be someone, somewhere, who might have seen the murderer entering either of the two flats or who was in the area of the Romney village of St Mary's-in-the-Marsh when the body of Caroline Pierce was dumped in a drainage ditch on 15 December 1987.

Possible clues that it is hoped will lead to an arrest are sets of missing keys that belong to the two victims. These, and small amounts of money, may have been taken from the two flats. The keys were fairly distinctive: Wendy Knell's had a 'Woman of the Year' tag whilst Caroline Pierce's had a tag from Buster Brown's, the American-style restaurant she managed in Camden Road.

Although the number of murders in Kent cannot be considered particularly high, it is a crime which, nevertheless, appears to be on the increase. Whilst in 1977 the number of recorded murders in the county stood at eleven, this figure had exactly doubled by 1987. However, it must also be admitted that these figures can fluctuate wildly, with 1980 recording only six murders. The latest figures, those for 1988, show a slight drop over the previous year, the number of recorded murders in the county standing at sixteen.

The fact that most murders committed within the county result in arrest and conviction is a direct reflection of the amount of time and effort expended on this particular crime. Upon a murder's first being reported, an incident room is established with a detective superintendent normally appointed to head the inquiry. If necessary, local detectives will be strengthened by members of the headquarters support staff, together with officers from other areas. Working in teams, these detectives will pursue certain aspects of the inquiry, such as investigating a shoeprint found at the scene of the crime or looking into the background of the victim.

Of particular importance is the need to carry out a detailed search of the area where the crime was committed or the body discovered. At this point any object or mark may prove to be of significance, and everything is carefully recorded and photographed before its removal and careful preservation. The usefulness of fingerprints has already been mentioned, but other evidence deposited by the murderer might well include blood, hair and urine. In each case, such items will be collected and then dispatched to the forensic laboratory at Aldermaston for analysis. Similarly, other laboratories are used for various other discoveries that might include spent bullets, cartridges or handwriting samples.

The help of a Home Office pathologist will also be enlisted, such a person not only determining the cause of death but also providing a wealth of additional information. Their particular expertise will allow them to indicate the type of weapon used and certain details pertinent to the identity of the murderer. The assistance of a Home Office pathologist is, of course, nothing new. Sir Bernard Spilsbury, invited to carry out an autopsy on Bessie Mundy and the three victims in the King's Wood shootings, was the first officially appointed Home Office pathologist, and Francis Camps also held this position.

Another expert sometimes asked to offer advice is a clinical psychologist. In the case of sex crimes or where excessive violence has been used, a psychologist may well be in a position to describe the type of person to be sought and whether further crimes of a similar nature might be expected. However, as one leading Kent police officer has been at pains to suggest, a clinical psychologist can sometimes be wrong, with evidence from the victim open to alternative explanations.

A further aid available to the county force in carrying out a murder inquiry is that of computers. For five years the Kent constabulary has been using AutoIndex, a versatile micro-computer package which can be adapted to any form of inquiry. However, for murder and other major crimes, the county police have acquired the Home Office Large Major Enquiry System (HOLMES), a standardized system which is being introduced throughout the whole country and allows for maximum co-operation between different forces which might well be involved in the same inquiry. Although it is not designed exclusively for the investigation of murders, the increasing frequency of this particular crime has resulted in its being used primarily in these investigations.

The need for a standardized system was particularly underlined as a result of numerous inadequacies identified during the 'Yorkshire Ripper' investigation. A Home Office report later indicated that not only had there been major errors of judgement but inefficiencies at various levels had been apparent. Most worrying was the inability of the various police forces involved to mount an effective synchronized inquiry. Since then, a number of reforms have been introduced into national police procedures that centre upon the adoption of a uniform strategy of approach. As part of this new strategy in the combating of crime, HOLMES is of outstanding importance. Not only does it mean that each force can more immediately share knowledge previously obtained by another but it also ensures less risk of unnecessary duplication of work undertaken.

The extent of police standardization does not stop with the actual computer system. Within the incident room itself the various personnel involved now have identical titles and identical duties. For those involved in the operation of HOLMES, this includes an office manager who is in overall charge, whilst a reader will be appointed to examine all documents, and an indexer records the movement of all information.

The application of HOLMES has already been tested in Kent through its use in several wide-ranging murder inquiries. Not least of these was that mounted in November 1988 following the disappearance of Derek Brann, a Folkestone taxi-driver whose body was subsequently discovered dumped next to the London-bound carriageway of the M20 near Sellindge.

As part of this inquiry Brann's red Nissan Bluebird taxi, found abandoned at the bottom of Horn Street in Seabrook, was taken to police headquarters at Maidstone, where it was completely stripped down. Samples of blood and other human debris were sent to Aldermaston for chemical analysis, whilst special attention was also given to the mud splashes around the wheel arches and on the bodywork. This last was considered of particular importance as it might help indicate exactly where the taxi had travelled during the hours prior to Brann's murder.

A major problem for any investigations involving a taxi concerns the large number of fare-paying passengers who would have been carried. On that busy Saturday night in which Brann was brutally stabbed to death, it is likely that thirty people would have been taken to a host of different destinations, each of them depositing hair, dust and fingerprints in and around the back seat of the taxi. To help eliminate those numerous innocent passengers, an appeal was put out for them to come forward, their prints being taken for the purpose of elimination.

With hundreds of people being interviewed and the chemical analyses providing further information about the murderer, all this information has to be stored in an easily retrievable state. This is where HOLMES comes into any inquiry, the computer having the memory and ability to hold thousands of seemingly unconnected pieces of information. When required, the computer can search its banks of received information, drawing links and comparisons that would take the ordinary human detective several weeks to match. It is, indeed, deserving of its name, but this particular Holmes is no fictional creation but a very real catcher of murderers and other criminals.

Although at the time of writing no arrest has been made in the case of the Tunbridge Wells or Derek Brann murders, the clear-up rate for this particular crime is extremely high. In fact, of the 153 murders reported in Kent between 1977 and 1987, a total of 145 (ninety-five per cent) have been solved. It is also more than likely that this high clear-up rate will continue. Most murders are carried out on the spur of the moment, with killers frequently leaving a mass of evidence that will lead to their later arrest. The few murderers who plan out their crime and attempt to conceal the evidence are just as likely to be caught. With the police making ever greater use of highly sophisticated equipment, the most unlikely object can be turned into a major clue as to the identity of the person they are seeking. Furthermore, even though a murder may appear to have been forgotten, the files are never closed. The slightest mistake made by the murderer may, even five or ten years later, result in an instant arrest. For this reason murderers, whether in Kent or anywhere else in the country, can never completely relax.

Appendix: *Scenes of the Crimes*

1. Robert Dadd. East side of Halfpence Lane approximately 0.2 miles north of the Cobham village war memorial. On early OS maps the hollow where the body was found is marked as Dadd's Hole.

2. Edward Walshe. Station master's office, Dover Priory station.

3. John Whibley. The infant school classroom, Biddenden village school. The classroom still exists, with the school now serving the needs of village children of primary school age. It is situated immediately opposite the parish church on the west side of the village.

4. Thomas and Ann Farrow. George Chapman's oil and paint store, 34 High Street, Deptford. The original shop still stands and carries the same High Street number.

5. Bessie Mundy. The Herne Bay house rented by George Joseph Smith, 80 The High Street (later re-numbered 159), has since been demolished. The site is now occupied by a 1930s-style shop.

6. Janie Swift, Janie and Peggy Stemp. East side of Kingswood Hill Road, 1.2 miles south of Challock Cross

Roads. The wall surrounding Eastwell Park still exists, and can be seen on the opposite side of the road. A gate standing opposite the site of the murder no longer exists.

7. Charlotte Saunders, Dorothy and Freda Fisher. Crittenden Cottage, Crittenden Lane, Matfield. This house has now been re-named and stands on the Crittenden Road, which links Matfield village with Colt's Hill. The house is sometimes referred to by local villagers as 'the murder house'.

8. PC Alan George Baxter. This murder was committed on the site of a former corporation rubbish dump that stood close to Sharsted (now Shawstead) Road between East Hill and Ham Lane.

9. Hubert Roderick and Alice Buxton. The lane leading to this cottage in Aldington is just off Frith Road.

Bibliography

Bishop, W.H., 'Murder in the Village School' in *Bygone Kent*, Vol. 9:8

Browne, D.G. and Tullett, E.V., *Bernard Spilsbury. His Life and Cases* (Harrap, 1951)

Cherrill, F., *Cherrill of the Yard* (Harrap, 1954)

du Rose, J., *Murder Was My Business* (Allen, 1971)

Honeycomb, G., *The Murders of the Black Museum* (Hutchinson, 1982)

La Bern, A., *Life and Death of a Ladykiller* (Frewin, 1967)

Laurence, J., *Seaside Crimes* (Marston, 1931)

Lyons, F. J., *George Joseph Smith* (Duckworth, 1935)

Notable British Trials Series:

Watson, E.R., *The Trial of George Joseph Smith*

Pierrepoint, A., *Executioner Pierrepoint* (Harrap, 1974)

Tullet, T., *Strictly Murder* (Bodley Head, 1979)

The files of the *Chatham News, Chatham Observer, Chatham Standard, Daily Mail, Daily Mirror, Dover Express, Illustrated Police Budget, Illustrated Police News, Isle of Thanet Gazette, Kentish Express, Kentish Independent, Kentish Mercury,* London *Evening Standard,* London *Evening Star,* Medway *Evening Post, Morning Worker, News Chronicle, Rochester, Chatham and Strood Gazette,* London *Times, Tonbridge Free Press.*

Index